ROYAL COURT

The Royal Court Theatre presents

NO QUARTER

by **Polly Stenham**

NO QUARTER was first performed at The Royal Court Jerwood Theatre Upstairs, Sloane Square, on Friday 11th January 2013.

NO QUARTER

by Polly Stenham

Cast in order of appearance
Robin **Tom Sturridge**
Oliver **Patrick Kennedy**
Lily **Maureen Beattie**
Coby **Alexa Davies**
Scout **Zoe Boyle**
Arlo **Joshua James**
Tommy **Taron Egerton**
Esme **Jenny Rainsford**

Director **Jeremy Herrin**
Designer **Tom Scutt**
Lighting Designer **Philip Gladwell**
Sound Designer **Fergus O'Hare**
Composer **Paul Englishby**
Casting Director **Amy Ball**
Assistant Director **Ned Bennett**
Design Associate **Fly Davis**
Production Managers **Tariq Rifaat & Emma Boyns**
Stage Managers **Alison Rich & Julia Slienger**
Stage Management Work Placements **John Lindus & Cariann Seeto**
Costume Supervisors **Iona Kenrick & Claire Wardroper**
Set built by **Richard Martin**

NO QUARTER is supported by the Royal College of Psychiatrists.

The Royal Court & Stage Management wish to thank the following for their help with this production: Young Vic, English Touring Theatre, Guildford School of Acting, National Youth Theatre, Almeida, British Heart Foundation, Chichester College, Southampton Nuffield, Donmar, Hampstead Theatre, Royal & Derngate, Oxfam Bookshop Kentish Town.

THE COMPANY

POLLY STENHAM (Writer)

FOR THE ROYAL COURT: Tusk Tusk, That Face.

AWARDS INCLUDE: Critics' Circle Award for Most Promising Playwright; Evening Standard Award for Most Promising Playwright; TMA Award for Best New Play (That Face).

In July 2012, Polly made her directorial debut by directing a staged reading of Look Back in Anger at the Duke of York's Theatre. Polly is currently under commission to the Donmar Warehouse and is writing a feature film adaptation of Tusk Tusk.

MAUREEN BEATTIE (Lily)

FOR THE ROYAL COURT: Waiting Room, Germany.

OTHER THEATRE INCLUDES: Enquirer, 27 (National Theatre of Scotland); The List, The Girls of Slender Means (Stellar Quines); The Master Builder (Chichester Festival); The Cherry Orchard, As You Like It, The Anatomist, Peer Gynt, Crime & Punishment, Edward II, The Tempest (Royal Lyceum); This Wide Night (Clean Break/Soho); Ghosts, Acting Up (Citizens'); Henry VI Part 2, Richard II, Richard III, Henry IV Parts 1 & 2, Henry V, Titus Andronicus, The Man Who Came to Dinner, Mary & Lizzie, King Lear, Macbeth, The Constant Couple (RSC); Medea (Theatre Babel/Edinburgh Festival Fringe/tour); Small Change, The Taming of the Shrew (Sheffield Crucible); Mother Goose (King's, Glasgow); Oedipus the Visionary (Theatre Babel); The Deep Blue Sea (Nottingham Playhouse); Candida (Theatre Royal, Plymouth/Salisbury Playhouse); Othello, The Merry Wives of Windsor (National); Damon & Pythias (Globe); Marie of Scotland (Edinburgh Festival Fringe/Tron); The Chinese Wolf (Bush); What Every Woman Knows (Scottish Theatre Company); Hard to Get, The Widows of Clyth (Traverse); The Innocents (Coventry); Ay Carmela (Contact); Ines de Castro (Riverside Studios); Othello (Lyric Hammersmith); Playboy of the Western World (Theatre Royal, Glasgow/Lyceum Little Theatre).

TELEVISION INCLUDES: Vera, Doctors, Moving On, Midsomer Murders, Lewis, The Worst Week of My Life, The Last Musketeer, Taggart, A Wing & A Prayer, City Central, Bramwell, Bad Girls, Ruffian Hearts, Boon, The Bill, Hard to Get, City Lights, The People Versus Scott, The Donegals, The Daftie, The Lost Tribe, The Campbells, The Long Roads, All Night Long, The Chief, Casualty.

FILM INCLUDES: Decoy Bride, Finding Bob MacArthur.

AWARDS INCLUDE: Manchester Evening News Theatre Award for Best Actress in a Visiting Production (Medea); Herald Angel Award (Medea); Pye Radio Award for Best Performance by an Actress (Can You Hear Me?).

NED BENNETT (Assistant Director)

AS DIRECTOR, THEATRE INCLUDES: Mercury Fur (Old Red Lion/Trafalgar Studios); Mr Noodles (Royal Exchange, Manchester); Blue Rabbits (Templeworks); Excellent Choice (Old Vic Tunnels); A Butcher of Distinction (King's Head); Edmond (Theatre Royal, Haymarket); Smartcard (Shunt Vaults); Selling Clive (Lost).

AS ASSISTANT DIRECTOR, THEATRE INCLUDES: Of Mice & Men (Watermill); A Letter to England (Finborough); Odette (Bridewell); Vent (Contact).

ZOE BOYLE (Scout)

THEATRE INCLUDES: Cat on a Hot Tin Roof (West Yorkshire Playhouse); Six Degrees of Separation (Old Vic); King Lear, The Seagull (RSC).

TELEVISION INCLUDES: Bad Girls (US pilot), Downton Abbey, Sons of Anarchy, Grey's Anatomy, Lewis, Poirot.

FILM INCLUDES: Freeloaders, King Lear.

ALEXA DAVIES (Coby)

Alexa is making her professional stage debut in No Quarter.

TELEVISION INCLUDES: New Tricks, Doctors, Little Cracker.

FILM INCLUDES: Vinyl, Bunking Off.

PAUL ENGLISHBY (Composer)

FOR THE ROYAL COURT: Sugar Mummies, Blood.

OTHER THEATRE INCLUDES: South Downs/The Browning Version (Chichester Festival); Hedda Gabler (Old Vic); The Orphan of Zhao, Written on the Heart, Cardenio, Twelfth Night, Hamlet, Love's Labour's Lost, A Midsummer Night's Dream (RSC); Children's Children, Marianne Dream (Almeida); The Thief of Baghdad, Pleasure's Progress (Royal Opera House); The Crane Maiden (Kanagawa).

TELEVISION INCLUDES: Dancing on the Edge, Luther, A Mother's Son, Good Cop, Inside Men, Outcasts, The Score, History of Football, Pictures on the Piano, Human Jungle, Hidden Voices, Living with the Enemy.

FILM INCLUDES: Sunshine on Leith, Page Eight, Hamlet, An Education, Miss Pettigrew Lives for a Day, Magicians, Confetti, An Englishman in New York, Ten Minutes Older – The Trumpet, Ten Minutes Older – The Cello, The Enlightenment, Serial Thriller, Death of the Revolution.

AWARDS INCLUDE: Emmy Award for Outstanding Original Main Title Theme Music (Page Eight).

TARON EGERTON (Tommy)

THEATRE INCLUDES: The Last of the Haussmans (National).

TELEVISION INCLUDES: Lewis.

PHILIP GLADWELL (Lighting Designer)

FOR THE ROYAL COURT: Oxford Street, Kebab.

OTHER THEATRE INCLUDES: Love The Sinner (National); Miss Julie (Schaubühne Berlin); God of Carnage, Blood Wedding, Hedda Gabler, The Bacchae (Royal & Derngate); Cinderella, Aladdin, Mogadishu, Punk Rock (Lyric Hammersmith); The Arthur Conan Doyle Appreciation Society, Melody, In The Bag (Traverse); The Spire, Design for Living (Salisbury Playhouse); Small Hours (Hampstead); For Once (Pentabus); Further Than the Furthest Thing (Dundee Rep); Five Guys Named Moe (Stratford East); Terminus (Abbey/world tour); You Can't Take it With You, 1984, Macbeth (Royal Exchange, Manchester); The Wiz (Birmingham Rep/West Yorkshire Playhouse); Thoroughly Modern Millie, Radio Times, Relatively Speaking, Daisy Pulls it Off, Blithe Spirit (Watermill); Gypsy, The King & I (Curve, Leicester); My Romantic History (Bush/Sheffield Crucible); Amazonia, Ghosts, The Member of the Wedding, Festa! (Young Vic); Testing the Echo (Out Of Joint); The Boy Who Fell Into a Book, Dandy in the Underworld (Soho).

AWARDS INCLUDE: Critics' Award for Theatre in Scotland for Best Design (Further Than the Furthest Thing).

JEREMY HERRIN (Director)

FOR THE ROYAL COURT: Hero, Haunted Child, The Heretic, Kin, Spur of the Moment, Off The Endz, The Priory, Tusk Tusk, The Vertical Hour, That Face (& Duke of York's).

OTHER THEATRE INCLUDES: This House, Statement of Regret (National); Absent Friends, Death & the Maiden (Harold Pinter); Uncle Vanya, South Downs (Chichester Festival); Much Ado About Nothing (Globe); Marble (Abbey, Dublin); The Family Reunion (Donmar); Blackbird (Market Theatre, Johannesburg); Sudden Collapses in Public Places, The Boy on the Swing, Gathered Dust & Dead Skin, The Lovers, Our Kind of Fun, Toast, Dirty Nets, Smack Family Robinson, Attachments, From the Underworld, The Last Post, Personal Belongings, ne1, Knives in Hens (Live).

FILM INCLUDES: Linked, Dead Terry, Warmth, Cold Calling.

RADIO INCLUDES: Flare Path, South Down, The Vertical Hour.

Jeremy is an Associate Director of the Royal Court.

JOSHUA JAMES (Arlo)

FOR THE ROYAL COURT: Love & Information.

TELEVISION INCLUDES: Whites, Silent Witness, Identity.

FILM INCLUDES: Summer In February.

PATRICK KENNEDY (Oliver)

THEATRE INCLUDES: The Glass Menagerie (Shared Experience); Measure for Measure (Theatre Royal, Plymouth/tour); Therese Raquin (National); Everything is Illuminated (Hampstead); Suddenly Last Summer (Sheffield Lyceum/Albany); A Midsummer Night's Dream, Les Liasons Dangereuses (Bristol Old Vic); Maps of Desire; A Clockwork Orange (Old Fire Station); Marge (Oxford Stage/Edinburgh Festival Fringe).

TELEVISION INCLUDES: Murder on the Home Front, Boardwalk Empire, Peep Show, Parade's End, Black Mirror: The National Anthem, Married Single Other, The 39 Steps, Consuming Passions, Einstein & Eddington, The Somme, Bleak House, Inspector Linley Mysteries, Cambridge Spies, Spooks.

FILM INCLUDES: War Horse, Pirates of the Caribbean: On Stranger Tides, Ourhouse, The Last Station, Me & Orson Welles, Atonement, In Transit, A Good Year, Mrs Henderson Presents, Munich, The Tulse Luper Suitcases, Nine Lives, Scratch.

FERGUS O'HARE (Sound Designer)

FOR THE ROYAL COURT: Red Bud, Presence, Credible Witness.

OTHER THEATRE INCLUDES: Arthur Conan Doyle Appreciation Society (Traverse); Opening Ceremony of the 2012 London Paralympic Games (Olympic Park, Stratford); Glasgow Girls, Macbeth (National Theatre of Scotland); Romeo & Juliet (Cork Opera House); A Chorus of Disapproval (Harold Pinter); Abigail's Party (Wyndham's/Menier/Theatre Royal, Bath); Henry V (Globe); Uncle Vanya (Minerva); Noises Off (Novello/Old Vic); All New People (Duke of York's); A Street Car Named Desire (Liverpool Playhouse); In The Next Room or The Vibrator Play (Theatre Royal, Bath); Macbeth (Lincoln Center); Hecuba, King Lear, The Seagull (BAM); Noises Off! (Brooks Atkinson); The Shape of Things (Promenade); A Day in the Death of Joe Egg (Roundabout); An Enemy of the People (Ahmanson); Rabbit (59E59); Electra (Barrymore).

JENNY RAINSFORD (Esme)

THEATRE INCLUDES: Straight (Sheffield/Bush); The Importance of Being Earnest (Rose, Kingston).

TELEVISION INCLUDES: Da Vinci's Demons.

FILM INCLUDES: **About Time, Prometheus.**

TOM SCUTT (Designer)

FOR THE ROYAL COURT: **Constellations, Remembrance Day.**

OTHER THEATRE INCLUDES: 13 (National); Absent Friends (West End); South Downs/The Browning Version (West End/Chichester Festival); The Lion, The Witch & The Wardrobe (Kensington Gardens); A Life of Galileo, The Merchant of Venice, Romeo and Juliet (RSC); The Weir (Donmar); King Lear, Through A Glass Darkly (Almeida); Hamlet (Sheffield Crucible); Realism (Soho); Mogadishu (Royal Exchange, Manchester/Lyric Hammersmith); Cinderella, Aladdin, Dick Whittington, Jack & The Beanstalk (Lyric Hammersmith); After Miss Julie (Salisbury Playhouse); The Contingency Plan: On the Beach/ Resilience (Bush); A Midsummer Night's Dream (Headlong); Edward Gant's Amazing Feats of Loneliness (Headlong /Soho); Vanya, Unbroken, The Internationalist (Gate); Bay (Young Vic); The Merchant of Venice (Octagon); Metropolis (Theatre Royal, Bath).

OPERA INCLUDES: Wozzeck (ENO – set); The Flying Dutchman (Scottish Opera); Rigoletto (OHP).

AWARDS INCLUDE: The Linbury Biennial Prize for Stage Design; The Jocelyn Herbert Award for Stage Design.

TOM STURRIDGE (Robin)

FOR THE ROYAL COURT: **Wastwater.**

OTHER THEATRE INCLUDES: **Punk Rock (Lyric Hammersmith/Royal Exchange, Manchester).**

TELEVISION INCLUDES: **Waste of Shame.**

FILM INCLUDES: **Effie, On The Road, Junkhearts, Waiting For Forever, The Boat That Rocked, Like Minds, Being Julia, Vanity Fair, Brothers of the Head.**

APPLAUDING
THE EXCEPTIONAL.

Coutts is proud to sponsor the Royal Court Theatre

THE ENGLISH STAGE COMPANY
AT THE ROYAL COURT THEATRE

'For me the theatre is really a religion or way of life. You must decide what you feel the world is about and what you want to say about it, so that everything in the theatre you work in is saying the same thing ... A theatre must have a recognisable attitude. It will have one, whether you like it or not.'

George Devine, first artistic director of the English Stage Company: notes for an unwritten book.

photo: Stephen Cummiskey

As Britain's leading national company dedicated to new work, the Royal Court Theatre produces new plays of the highest quality, working with writers from all backgrounds, and addressing the problems and possibilities of our time.

"The Royal Court has been at the centre of British cultural life for the past 50 years, an engine room for new writing and constantly transforming the theatrical culture." Stephen Daldry

Since its foundation in 1956, the Royal Court has presented premieres by almost every leading contemporary British playwright, from John Osborne's Look Back in Anger to Caryl Churchill's A Number and Tom Stoppard's Rock 'n' Roll. Just some of the other writers to have chosen the Royal Court to premiere their work include Edward Albee, John Arden, Richard Bean, Samuel Beckett, Edward Bond, Leo Butler, Jez Butterworth, Martin Crimp, Ariel Dorfman, Stella Feehily, Christopher Hampton, David Hare, Eugène Ionesco, Ann Jellicoe, Terry Johnson, Sarah Kane, David Mamet, Martin McDonagh, Conor McPherson, Joe Penhall, Lucy Prebble, Mark Ravenhill, Simon Stephens, Wole Soyinka, Polly Stenham, David Storey, Debbie Tucker Green, Arnold Wesker and Roy Williams.

"It is risky to miss a production there." Financial Times

In addition to its full-scale productions, the Royal Court also facilitates international work at a grass roots level, developing exchanges which bring young writers to Britain and sending British writers, actors and directors to work with artists around the world. The research and play development arm of the Royal Court Theatre, The Studio, finds the most exciting and diverse range of new voices in the UK. The Studio runs play-writing groups including the Young Writers Programme, Critical Mass for black, Asian and minority ethnic writers and the biennial Young Writers Festival. For further information, go to www.royalcourttheatre.com/playwriting/the-studio.

"Yes, the Royal Court is on a roll. Yes, Dominic Cooke has just the genius and kick that this venue needs... It's fist-bitingly exciting." Independent

Jerwood Theatre Downstairs

Until 19 Jan 2013

in the republic of happiness by Martin Crimp

A provocative roll-call of contemporary obsessions.

15 Feb – 9 Mar 2013

if you don't let us dream, we won't let you sleep by Anders Lustgarten

A new play exploding the ethos of austerity and offering an alternative.
Part of the Royal Court's Jerwood New Playwrights programme, supported by the Jerwood Charitable Foundation.

21 Mar – 27 Apr 2013

the low road by Bruce Norris

A fable of free market economics and cut-throat capitalism.

Jerwood Theatre Upstairs

22 Feb – 23 Mar 2013

a time to reap by Anna Wakulik translated by Catherine Grosvenor

An exciting new voice looking at Poland's hottest political topics
– abortion and the Catholic Church.
International Playwrights: A Genesis Foundation Project.

5 Apr – 4 May 2013

a new play written and directed by Anthony Neilson

Renowned for his ground-breaking new work, Anthony Neilson
returns to the Royal Court.

17 – 26 Jan 2013

rough cuts

New work exploring our relationship
to the internet.

The Studio is supported by The Andrew Lloyd
Webber Foundation. *Rough Cuts* is supported
by the Columbia Foundation Fund of the
London Community Foundation.

Wilson Rehearsal Studio, Royal Court

25 Jan – 23 Feb

feast

a new play by **Yunior García Aguilera**
(Cuba), **Rotimi Babatunde** (Nigeria),
Marcos Barbosa (Brazil), **Tanya Barfield**
(US), **Gbolahan Obisesan** (UK)

A Young Vic and Royal Court production
Part of World Stages London

Young Vic Theatre, SE1 8LZ

020 7565 5000
www.royalcourttheatre.com

⊖ Sloane Square ⇌ Victoria ☐ royalcourt ☐ theroyalcourttheatre

Principal Sponsor **Coutts**

**ARTS COUNCIL
ENGLAND**

ROYAL COURT SUPPORTERS

The Royal Court has significant and longstanding relationships with many organisations and individuals who provide vital support. It is this support that makes possible its unique playwriting and audience development programmes.

Coutts is the Principal Sponsor of the Royal Court. The Genesis Foundation supports the Royal Court's work with International Playwrights. Theatre Local is sponsored by Bloomberg. The Jerwood Charitable Foundation supports new plays by playwrights through the Jerwood New Playwrights series. The Andrew Lloyd Webber Foundation supports the Royal Court's Studio, which aims to seek out, nurture and support emerging playwrights.

The Harold Pinter Playwright's Award is given annually by his widow, Lady Antonia Fraser, to support a new commission at the Royal Court.

PUBLIC FUNDING
Arts Council England, London
British Council
European Commission Representation in the UK

CHARITABLE DONATIONS
Martin Bowley Charitable Trust
Columbia Foundation Fund of the London Community Foundation
Cowley Charitable Trust
The Dorset Foundation
The John Ellerman Foundation
The Eranda Foundation
Genesis Foundation
J Paul Getty Jnr Charitable Trust
The Golden Bottle Trust
The Haberdashers' Company
Jerwood Charitable Foundation
Marina Kleinwort Charitable Trust
The Andrew Lloyd Webber Foundation
John Lyon's Charity
The Andrew W. Mellon Foundation
The David & Elaine Potter Foundation
Rose Foundation
The Royal College of Psychiatrists
Royal Victoria Hall Foundation
The Dr Mortimer & Theresa Sackler Foundation
John Thaw Foundation
The Vandervell Foundation
The Garfield Weston Foundation

CORPORATE SUPPORTERS & SPONSORS
BBC
Bloomberg
Coutts
Ecosse Films
Kudos Film & Television
MAC
Moët & Chandon
Oakley Capital Limited
Smythson of Bond Street
White Light Ltd

BUSINESS ASSOCIATES, MEMBERS & BENEFACTORS
Annouska
Auerbach & Steele Opticians
Bank of America Merrill Lynch
Byfield Consultancy
Hugo Boss
Lazard
Savills
Troy Asset Management
Vanity Fair

DEVELOPMENT ADVOCATES
John Ayton MBE
Elizabeth Bandeen
Kinvara Balfour
Anthony Burton CBE
Piers Butler
Sindy Caplan
Sarah Chappatte
Cas Donald (Vice Chair)
Celeste Fenichel
Emma Marsh (Chair)
Deborah Shaw Marquardt (Vice Chair)
Tom Siebens
Sian Westerman
Nick Wheeler
Daniel Winterfeldt

Principal Sponsor

 Supported by
ARTS COUNCIL ENGLAND

No Quarter

Polly Stenham's plays include *That Face* (Royal Court and the Duke of York's), for which she was awarded the 2008 Critics' Circle Award for Most Promising Playwright, the *Evening Standard* Award for Most Promising Playwright 2007 and TMA Best New Play 2007, *Tusk Tusk* (Royal Court) and *Hotel California* (Latitude).

also by Polly Stenham from Faber

THAT FACE
TUSK TUSK

POLLY STENHAM

No Quarter

ff

faber and faber

This edition first published in 2013
by Faber and Faber Limited
74–77 Great Russell Street, London WC1B 3DA

The right of Polly Stenham to be identified as author
of this work has been asserted in accordance with Section 77
of the Copyright, Designs and Patents Act 1988

A CIP record for this book
is available from the British Library

Typeset by Country Setting, Kingsdown, Kent CT14 8ES
Printed and bound by CPI Group (UK) Ltd, Croydon, CR0 4YY

ISBN 978-0-571-30179-9

2 4 6 8 10 9 7 5 3 1

For Anne

1955–2012

Characters

Robin
twenty-four

Oliver
thirty-four

Lily
early sixties

Coby
fourteen

Tommy
nineteen

Scout
twenty-five

Arlo
twenty-five

Esme
twenty-four

NO QUARTER

Act One

Present day. Winter. Afternoon. The drawing room of a remote country house.

The room has a shabby glory. Large double doors lead out into the garden. There is a piano, a sofa, and a battered armchair. Shelves are lined with books. The house has been restored and rebuilt by Lily. Certain details reflect this. There are two side doors. One exits to the kitchen, the other to the rest of the house.

The curtains are drawn. The room dim. Over the scene the sky outside darkens to dusk.

Robin stands in the centre of the room, barefoot. He lights a cigarette. There is a sudden banging at the door. Robin turns slowly.

Oliver (*off*) Robin? ROBIN.

Robin doesn't react. More banging.

I know you're in there. I saw the car.

More banging.

Robin smokes the last of his cigarette. He stubs it out carefully. He pours a drink from the bar and takes a sip. He rests the glass on the piano. He takes a breath and turns to the rattling door. It is bolted shut. Robin unlocks it.

ROBIN, OPEN THE FUCKING DOOR!

Robin flings open the door. Oliver is revealed. He is older than Robin by a decade. He wears a crumpled suit and loosened tie. He is holding the door handle.

Is she here?

Robin Who?

Oliver Lily. Mum. Our mother. Is she here?

Robin Mum? Yikes. No. Should she be?

Robin seems drunk. Thick with it.

Oliver Are you absolutely sure?

Robin Yes, I'm sure. Why . . . so . . . serious?

Oliver She's missing. From the care home. Again.

Robin Is that all? Oh relax. She'll turn up. She did last time.

Oliver I know but –

Robin And the time before. (*Slurs.*) No need to get your suit in a twist.

Beat.

It's Tuesday. No. Thursday. No. Definitely Tuesday. Maybe it's even Friday. Is it Friday?

Oliver Oh, forget it.

Robin Shouldn't you be in London anyway? I thought you had a . . . vote. Or did the Tree House give you the day off? As it's a Friday and all.

Oliver It's a fucking Tuesday.

Robin I knew it. Always go with your first instinct.

Oliver How did you know I had a vote?

Robin I follow it sometimes. Always fun to see the big bro on the box. You look so tiny. Like an angry thumb. But look. Here you are. In all your life-size glory. A little field trip to the country, is it? Got your packed lunch?

Oliver Shut up.

Robin I must say it's very exotic to have you down these parts. Now that you're so urbane. MP for Ilford North no less. Do they have –

Oliver I think you mean urban.

Robin What?

Oliver *Urban*, not urbane.

Robin Do they have any idea, your 'constituents', what 'manor'. Actual. Literal. Manor. You spring from?

Oliver I'm not getting into this again, Robin, it's boring and it's irrelevant. Look, if she –

Robin It's a twisting irony that after so many years of people trying to ferret their way up the socio-economic scale, you would like nothing more than to slither all the way down it. Do you adopt an accent in Ilford North, 'blud'? I bet the Tree House encourages it . . .

Oliver If she turns up here go to the payphone in the village. But walk. Don't drive. I'll leave my numbers here. I presume your mobile is still in the Thames?

> *Robin shrugs.*
> *Oliver sets the door handle down. Robin pounces on it.*

Robin You brute, you broke it. You pulled too hard.

Oliver It's a door handle, you're meant to pull hard.

Robin I'll fix it, give it here.

Oliver This place is falling apart.

Robin No it's not.

Oliver The roof is sagging, I saw from the drive.

Robin Don't say that. It's cruel.

Oliver To whom?

Robin The house.

He lights a cigarette, swaying a little.

Oliver It's a building, not a person. Why the hell are you back here anyway? Isn't it term time?

Robin taps ash provocatively on to the floor.

This pace is a tinderbox, Robin, do not be a –

Robin does it again.

PRICK. Give me that.

He grabs the cigarette off Robin and chucks it outside.

Oliver It's the middle of the week. Don't you have classes? Don't you have something, anything else to do –

Robin I'm working actually. I'm composing a theme tune.

Oliver You've come all the way up here to –

Robin I like the quiet. And someone has to take care of the place after you put her in the little-old-lady prison, we can't leave it unmanned. It's our land.

Oliver It's the best care home in the county, Robin; I will not go through this again.

Robin It's a little old lady prison and you know it . . . Now if you don't mind I must start composing.

Oliver A theme tune to what exactly?

Robin My fantastic life, now sod off.

Oliver Hold on . . . I get it. You finally got kicked out, didn't you?

Robin I left actually.

Oliver That's why you're back here in the middle of term. Ran home to the castle. Reinstalled yourself. Glass in one hand. Cock in another.

Robin I was *not* kicked out.

Beat.

We came to a mutual agreement.

Oliver Well done. One hand clapping in a fucking forest yet again.

Robin heads to the bar. He stands so that he is blocking the closed kitchen door. He pours a drink.

What are you doing?

Robin I'm water-skiing, what does it look like?

Oliver It's two in the . . . Oh forget it.

Robin Well, as it's your day off, why don't you join me?

Oliver I hate how you make me this person. This person who has to nag you. To tell you off. I am not this fucking person –

Robin We could go fishing. Shooting even. Hold on. I forgot you renounced all that. Tree-house rules.

Oliver STOP CALLING IT THAT. The House of Commons is not a fucking tree house.

Beat.

Robin Well it sort of is . . . if you think about it . . . boys with their toys . . . up high.

Oliver I said to myself. On the way up. If you were here, we weren't going to do this. And we're not. We're just not. OK? (*Almost to himself.*) I should have insisted on a phone here.

Robin Off you trot then. I'll let you know if she turns up.

Oliver has taken off his tie and balled it in his hand during the last sequence. He absent-mindedly leaves it on the sofa. He starts looking for something.

Oliver If you don't pass out first. And let me know how exactly? By fucking carrier pigeon? Can you even get to the payphone in the village this pissed? Where are your shoes?

Robin I don't like shoes.

Oliver How bohemian of you.

Robin I find them restricting. We were not born in tiny shoes.

Robin stares out of the garden doors.

It's almost more beautiful in winter. The land. Starker. The trees are . . . all angles.

He cocks his head.

Robin Hold on. Can you hear that?

Oliver What?

Robin I can hear it really faintly . . . I think it's . . . hold on, is it faint crying?

Oliver Where? Who?

Robin I hear faint mewling . . . I think it's the state crying for its nanny . . . Time to go, don't you think?

Oliver Oh get a job, Robin.

Robin I work, you skunk, I write. Just because I don't have a fucking desk.

Oliver gives him a withering look. He then spies what he was looking for. It is a clay mouse. Made by a child. He handles it delicately.
Robin shoves some pages of music at Oliver.

Look.

Oliver Yes. Because playing the piano on your own. To yourself. In the middle of nowhere. Is a very serious important job, Robin. It's so very useful.

Beat.
  He looks at him properly.

This place holds you back. It's sad actually. When you can run back here you'll never –

Robin Enter the fray? Give a shit. Have you seen the fray lately? I reject the fray.

Oliver Or did it reject you?

Robin What did you say?

Oliver Don't get too used to it up here, princeling. Remember it's not just your house and it never will be.

Robin (*notices the mouse*) What are you doing with that?

Oliver I'm taking it to give Lily. For her room. Maybe there are some other things I should bring if I'm here. Her room is a bit. Sparse. Some books maybe. Something to cheer her up when we find her. Which we will.

  He heads to the kitchen door. Robin blocks him.

Robin I made that mouse.

Oliver No. You didn't. I did.

Robin No. I did. Out of clay. I did –

Oliver It's the only bloody thing I made her in my life. It was year four. It took me ages. It's mine.

Robin Let me see it.

Oliver It was after her first mouse book was published. You weren't even born.

Robin No. That is definitely one of mine.

Oliver You were home-schooled, how the hell would you have made it, you didn't exactly have art classes –

Robin Give it!

Oliver Look, I even signed it. Here. Olly. With a Y.

Robin grabs the mouse off Oliver. He drops it. It smashes.
Silence.
Oliver is battling to compose himself. He just wins.

That was the only thing I ever made her.

Pause.
He picks up his car keys.

If she turns up. Call me. The numbers are here.

Robin nods.

Please don't drive.

Oliver makes to go.

Robin Ollie?

His voice is different.
Oliver turns.

Oliver What?

Small pause. He doesn't want him to go.

Robin Fuck off then.

Oliver exits.
Robin goes to the windows to watch him go. He locks the doors. His body language straightens out. He isn't drunk.
The kitchen door opens. Lily is standing there. She is wearing a hand-made Cleopatra mask and a silk dressing gown.
Robin stares at her. He takes a breath.

You changed I see. Goodo.

He goes to help her into the room. She bats him off.

You listened, didn't you? I told you not listen. Now you're upset.

Lily It's very hot in here.

Robin You do know you have a mask on, Lily.

Lily Don't be patronising, Christopher. It doesn't suit you.

She pulls off the mask.

It was a joke. I was lightening the tone. That's the problem with losing your bloody mind, no one knows when you're being funny. It's wound in the salt. The final indignity. Not being allowed to be fucking hilarious.

Small pause. Her tone changes entirely.

I couldn't find the rest of the costume. It must be in the box.

She gestures to the birthday box, a locked chest in the corner of the room.

But where is the key? The key . . . I know I hid it somewhere.

She starts looking around the room.

Robin (*to himself*) OK. Right. That was fine with Oliver, wasn't it? Was it? Was it fine?

He fumbles for a cigarette. He lights one.

Or was it a colossal fuck-up?

Lily Don't swear.

Robin Right. Let's think. He believed I was pissed. I'll have to just. Let him think. I'll have to say . . . I passed out upstairs. That I was so drunk I missed you arrive. That's the only. Option really. Christ.

19

Beat.

He'll hate me.

Lily He does already.

Robin Gee whizz, Lily, thank you. And I would like to thank you again for choosing me for the job. It is just lashings of fun. Honestly.

Lily It's OK.

Robin (*flash of upset*) Is it?

She is crouched on the floor looking through a lower bookshelf. She nods. Their eyes meet. She keeps looking for the key. Talking as she does.

Lily But it has to be our secret.

Robin I am aware of that, yes.

Lily (*suddenly agitated, loud*) BECAUSE IT'S VERY IMPORTANT TO ME THAT HE DOESN'T THINK HE COULD STOP. THAT HE COULD HAVE STOPPED.

Robin (*mildly but as loud*) I get it, Lily.
What are you looking for?

Lily . . .

She can't remember. Horrible pause. He changes tack quickly.

Robin Let's have a cigarette. Oh shit, we're nearly out. Was there another pack in the car? Probably not. Here. Let's share this one.

He comes to sit next to her. He lights the fag. They pass it back and forth. She rests her head on his shoulder.

Do fags have different tastes, like wine?

Lily I suppose they do.

Robin Could you have a fag-tasting like a wine-tasting? Why do people not do that?

Suddenly an alarm goes off. It is the 'Pink Panther' theme tune.
Robin stands up and goes to the shelf to switch it off. Next to the alarm are a bottle of pills and a yogurt. He prepares the dose as he talks calmly.

You know the weirdest thing happened when I drove up to get you. I was waiting by the hedge. You, as you well know, were late. I started to panic a bit. Thought I was in the wrong spot. So I was poring over the map. And when I looked up, guess who was sitting on the bonnet of the car, and I swear I'm not making this up.

Small pause.

Lily God.

Robin How did you know?

He hands her the pills and yogurt. She starts taking them.

Lily Oh, I see God all the time. I pat the air to freak the nurses out.

Robin You evil bitch.

Lily grins.

When I glanced back he had gone. I miss that cat. Here. Water.

She takes a sip.
He sniffs the air.

Oh shit. It's burning.

He pelts offstage. When he is gone Lily picks up Oliver's tie. She twists it in her hands and smells it. She closes her eyes. She hears Robin returning. She quickly puts it down.

Robin enters with a wheeled table set for two. He whips off a silver cloche to reveal a roast chicken. Burnt almost black.

Lily looks at the chicken then slowly looks up at him. She raises an eyebrow.

Lily It's . . . you've . . . it's . . .

Her mouth moves. She is struggling to find the right word.

Nigger.

Robin Sorry what?

Lily It's –

Robin Black. Black because it's burnt? What you meant was burnt.

Beat.

Don't say that word. Even if you're –

Lily Fuck this. FUCK IT. Words. Slip. Change as I think them. Not all the time but –

She looks up, suddenly tearful.

Robin (*softly*) Mulligrub . . .

Lily Smatchet.

Lily Fuckweasel, cockmuppet, clapper-clawed tit hound.

Robin Ooo la la . . . How about . . . bescumber.

Lily Bint.

Robin Good. Solid. Cunt?

Beat.

Lily Pedestrian.

She pokes the chicken and starts to laugh. Robin stares at her for a moment then turns away. He takes a breath.

Let's just have a drink. A last meal was a bit of an odd concept anyway. A bit . . . Texan as a notion. I want to die thin anyway.

Robin composes himself and uncorks a bottle of wine. He pours two glasses. He is about to hand her one when he freezes.

Robin Hold on. It said not to mix any of it with booze.

Lily I don't care.

Robin You can have water.

Lily No.

Robin If you're sick we'll have to start again. You might have to go to hospital.

Lily Twat-bandit.

Robin That's not funny any more. Here. Water.

Lily I'm not a dog.

Robin Then stop acting like a bitch.

Lily I. Want it.

Small pause. They stare at each other. She picks up the wine glass. Her hand is shaking. She raises the glass as if to toast.

Robin Have half, please.

Lily sips the wine. Pleasure floods her face.

Lily Heaven. Real heaven. Not having your soul fingered – (*Sips again.*) By a gigantic . . . sky wizard. Stupid idea. STUPID IDEA. MOST STUPID IDEA I EVER HEARD. Stupid. And camp when you think about it. Someone's going to die. Quick. Perfume. Capes. Music.

Pause.

I want some music.

Robin (*quietly*) I want a cigarette.

She goes to the record player. He watches her. She struggles but she manages to play a record.
Lily turns and grins. Robin hangs his head. When he looks up he smiles. The song has history for them. She dances for him. She beckons him towards her. He gets up. They dance close to each other. She starts to tire. He puts her feet on his so he can move for them both. She rests her head on his shoulder.
She leans into Robin more heavily. He guides her back on to the sofa. Lily picks up Oliver's tie.

Robin Chocolate? I got your favourite?

Lily My husband forgot his tie.

Robin It's Oliver's tie, Lily.

Lily Has he left for the office?

Robin Oliver?

Lily Gideon. Oliver doesn't wear a tie.

Robin Oh, these days he does.

Lily GIDEON?

Robin straightens up. He realises she's hallucinating.

I need to find my husband. He can't go to work without a tie.

She tries to stand.

Robin (*calm*) Lily. Back in the room. Come on. Look at me. Back here. Please. Pull yourself back.

Lily I need to speak to my husband.

She doesn't seem to know who he is. Her eyes slip all over him.

Robin Gideon is dead, Lily. He died twenty-three years ago.

Her eyes widen.

I'm Robin your youngest son. My father Gideon is dead. I didn't know him.

She touches his face.

Lily Oh. (*Slowly, carefully.*) How did he die?

Robin He had been away. On business. And he missed us. So on his way home he drove too fast. It had been snowing. The car crashed. He died.

Beat.
    Lily is visibly upset. Her face twists.

Lily Snow.

Robin It was a long time ago. Just one square. For me.

She takes the chocolate. It is hard for her to eat. Long pause.

(*Softly.*) I would punch a baby for a cigarette. Should have got packs. Packs and packs. Should have thought that through. If I had some now I'd smoke three at once. Two up the nose. One in the mouth. Each a different brand.
    You look pale. Maybe you should have another anti-nausea.

Lily I don't feel sick. I feel . . . wavy.

Robin Shall we sit still then? If you're waving.

He settles next to her and tries to hold her hand. She moves hers away.

Lily I'd rather not.

Robin Hold my bloody hand.

Lily I don't like to. I've never liked to. Makes me think of awkwardness at the cinema. No one really likes to hold hands, I'm sure. They sweat.

Robin Lots of people like to hold hands.

Lily Do they though? Actually?

Robin Just do it.

She does. They sit still for a moment. Suddenly Robin springs up.

I can't.

Lily Hold hands. I know. It's a bit forced, isn't it?

Robin No. I can't . . .

Lily just stares at him.

Lily We. Made. A. Deal.

He shakes his head.

I jump. I choose.

Robin But I don't have a fucking choice in this, do I? You knew I couldn't bear the alternative. You. Trying. Somewhere. Alone. Fucking it up maybe. Ending up . . . Oh fuck. Oh fuck

Pause. He is shaking.
He looks at her.

Robin If we make you sick –

Lily No. No. No. We're not stopping. Look at the paper. The PLAN. What I wrote to do. No. I REFER YOU TO THE FUCKING PLAN.

Robin I need to stick my fingers down your throat.

Lily Do you fuck.

> *She scrambles away from him.*
> *The Pink Panther alarm goes off again.*

FUCKING GET THEM. I WILL NOT GO BACK
THERE, YOU UNDERSTAND. THE HUMILIATION.
But I WILL NOT. I WILL NOT. Be so. DEGRADED.
Understand, boy? You don't die of this. You die before
you die. SOMEONE WIPES YOUR ARSE. You fucking
PISS YOURSELF. Let. Me. Choose.

Robin You could move back here. I could live with you.
We could –

Lily NO.

Lily It will be all right.

Robin No. No, it won't.

> *She tries to get the pills herself. It is horrible to watch.*
> *She falls. She turns away from him on the floor.*
> *Robin picks up the tie. He hooks it over his neck.*
> *He kneels to help her up.*
> *She burrows into his neck for a moment. Her hands*
> *find the tie. When she looks up she is hallucinating*
> *again.*

Lily We should have never married.

Robin Lily?

Lily Always so good at being quiet, Gideon. Sickeningly
good.

> *He tries to move away, but she clings to the tie.*

Lily It's aggression really. Quietness. Anger in a mime
suit. So fucking English.

Robin Look at my face. Look right at my face. It's me. Robin. Come on. Come back. Come on.

Lily Robin?

Robin Yes.

Lily He doesn't even look like you.

Robin What?

Lily Admit it, Gideon. It's fucking *obvious*.

Robin What are you talking about, Lily?

Lily I like a margarita, but one at the very most, three I'm under the table, four I'm under the . . . host . . .

Horrible pause.

Rat got your tongue? Even you, Gideon, must have something to say to that . . .

Robin Stop this, stop it.

Lily He never did look like you, did he? From the moment he was born. He was just mine. Your wooden nickel. Just mine.

Robin FUCKING STOP IT.

Lily You knew, admit it

Lily That's more like it.

Robin Please . . .

Lily Much more like it.

Small pause.

Robin You . . . bitch.

Lily I like you like this. I like it. Some life in you, some fight.

28

Pause.

Kiss me.

Robin pushes her away.

Kiss me or GO. Be a MAN and GO!

Robin MUMMY, SNAP OUT OF IT!

Lily leans in to kiss him.

I'm ROBIN.

Lily Shhh . . . He's asleep, I checked on them.

She tries again. Robin slaps her. She falls back on to the sofa. After a moment she pulls herself up again. There is a dark stain on her robe. She sits down. They catch their breath.
  He makes the decision. Slowly he stands up and takes the last dose from the shelf. He sits next to her. She manages the pills in two gulps.
  Small pause.

Don't be mulligrubs, my mulligrub.

Pause.

Robin So I've seen God and you've seen God. Maybe he didn't die.

Lily Don't be ridiculous. We ran him over.

Robin Oh yeah.

They grin at each other. She turns away. After a moment she takes his hand and holds it. They sit still for a moment. Robin spots something under the piano. He darts to get it. He picks up an old fag packet. There are two fags left.

Robin Bingo. One each. Lily?

No reply.

Mummy . . .

He shakes her shoulder. Nothing. He checks her breathing. She is alive but unconscious. It has begun.
He takes her instructions and burns them with a lighter. He takes a note from the table. He opens it and without reading the letter he chucks it on to the piano. His breathing is jagged, he needs air.
He flings open the garden doors. A girl is standing there. He slams them shut.

Coby (*off*) Well that was rude –

He locks it.

Coby (*off*) Robin? ROBIN!

Robin (*under his breath*) Shit shit shit.

She tries to open the door.

Coby (*off*) You've locked it? I can get in other ways, you know, the kitchen window's open.

Robin Shit.

He covers Lily completely with a blanket, his jacket, in a mad impulse scatters some cushions over her.

Coby(*off*) What are you *doing*?

Robin It locks itself. Just a second.

He tries to compose himself, counts to three, then opens the door.
A fourteen-year-old girl, Coby, is revealed. She is scruffy. Tomboy. A local girl he's known for ever.

Coby Why are you being so weird?

Robin Coby, this is not a good time –

Coby I was just passing. Thought you might fancy a spliff –

Robin Coby please –

Coby I've got the best weed, you know –

Robin Not right now –

Coby Why didn't you call? . . . You always call when you're back –

She turns to the door, the key is in the lock.

It doesn't just lock itself. You *lied.*

She holds up the key.

Keys don't just turn on their own now do they? Not old-fashioned ones like that.

Robin I must have done it automatically.

Coby (*dry*) Sure . . .

Beat.

You've got a girl here, haven't you . . .

Robin Not exactly. Look, Coby –

Coby You do, don't you? You're so bad. I thought you were going out with that twin, what's her name, Scout. Is it her? Are you hiding her . . . Funny . . .

Robin No. Look, there's no one here.

Coby Then why is there a table set for two?

Robin Coby, just fuck off would you?

Coby I wrote you something.

Robin Thanks, that's very sweet but –

She shoves him a bit of crumpled paper from her pocket.

Coby To set to music. It's a song. It might not be very good but. Well, you said you always had trouble with lyrics and –

Coby absent-mindedly puts the key on the bookshelf

Robin You need to go now. Go on. Off you go.

She dawdles

Fuck OFF, Coby.

Coby Do you want them or not?I mean will you actually read them? They took me ages and I don't have a copy so if you don't want them, give them back, there are bands at school you know, like three.

Robin Have them back then. Here.

Coby Oh.

She looks like she's about to cry. Robin sneaks a look back at Lily. At this moment her hand slips out and dangles into view.

Robin Coby . . .

Coby It's just. I wrote them for you. They're about you.

Robin I'll keep them then. Thank you. Off you go now.

He is steering her out of the door.

Coby Bye . . .

He shuts the doors and pulls the curtains. He searches for the key. He can't see it. Just as he finds it on the shelf, Coby shoves the doors back open.

Robin, I love you.

She sees the hand.

Oh my . . . SHIT. Who –

She panics, Robin wraps her in a bear hug. She struggles.

Robin STOP IT, AND I'LL LET GO. Please. Please Coby. Shhh . . . I'll explain, OK. I'll explain.

She stops. He releases her, she backs away from him. She is breathing hard.

Coby Who . . . is . . . that?

Robin It's not what it –

Coby WHO?

Robin It's Lily.

Coby Lily . . .

Robin Yes.

Coby What's wrong with her, Robin?

Robin You know how she got sick. Really sick. Quickly. Couldn't remember stuff –

Coby Yes –

Robin And Oliver had her sent to the home. Even though she didn't want to go –

Coby Yes –

Robin Well. She decided . . .

It dawns on her.

Coby That's wrong.

Robin No it's not.

Coby It fucking is. You're messing with nature. Hubris. This is fucking hubris.

Robin Big word. Learn it at school?

Coby Don't be a cunt.

Robin My point is you're fourteen so it's going to be hard for you to understand this but please, I'm begging you to listen to me because you can stop it all now if you want to, and that would really fuck things up, Coby. Really fucking fuck things up. If you tell someone, if people know that I was here. There will be a court case. An investigation. There's a house at stake. Stuff to inherit. She'll have left the place to me. So it'll look terrible. It'll look like I . . . And I promised her, I swore that Oliver wouldn't find out that I helped. Because he can't think he could have stopped it. That was her last wish. She wanted to protect him from any pain and any scandal. If you tell he'll be smeared. It'll be in the papers. There will be a mess. A big, ugly, inky mess.

Coby And if I don't?

Robin I'll put your lyrics in a song.

Beat.

That was a joke.

Coby It was hilarious.

Robin What are you going to do?

Coby I don't know.

Small pause.

Robin I thought you loved me.

Coby I'm fourteen, I think I love everyone.

Robin Fucking decide.

Small pause.

Coby Kiss me.

Robin Excuse me?

Coby Kiss me just once and I'll go.

Robin What? Why?

Coby Because I want to know what it feels like.

Robin You opportunistic little shit. You'll go far.

Coby Go on then.

Robin goes to her. The moment is unsure. Clumsy. Confused. But it happens.

I knocked but. Nothing.

She walks over to Lily. Then turns to Robin.

She was wild. She shouldn't be in hospital. It would be like a cage.

Beat.

Let me do one thing.

Robin nods.
Coby pelts out of the door and returns in a flash. She is holding a winter flower.
She lays it on the blanket.

She loved the land.

She tears up.

You're not going to leave here, are you? Now this place is sold. You could stay with me.

Robin What?

Coby I thought you'd sold it. My aunt said. I didn't believe her but –

Robin I'm staying right here.

Coby They came sniffing to us first, but we can't sell the farm. Want the land for a golf course or something. They went to your mum next.

Robin No. That's not true. That can't be true.

Coby Lily told her she did. Auntie was surprised because it was such a low offer but –

Robin You're. Wrong.

Coby Good. So you're not going anywhere? Promise.

He shakes his head.

Never?

Robin Never.

Coby I never would have told, you know. I do love you.

Beat.

You're wild too.

She darts out of the door.
  Blackout.

Act Two

Six weeks later. Robin's birthday. Night.
The stage is dark. A figure smashes the door from
outside. It crashes open. The figure enters, hood up. An
alarm starts to wail. The figure turns on the light and
snaps the alarm off. He pulls down his hood. It is Robin.
He slings his top off. Underneath he is wearing a dark
three-piece suit. He has the beginnings of a black eye and
some blood on his sleeve. He holds an axe and brightly
wrapped present. He set the axe down and places the
present on the piano.

The room is shabbier, scuzzier. Exactly half the
furnishings have gone. The heating and hot water have
been cut off. A portable heater sits next to a makeshift
bed. There are several cans of paint and tools stacked in
a corner, and what looks like a crossbow nearby. The
birthday box remains as it was. There is now a stack of
musical instruments by the piano. Ranging from
traditional (violin) and modern (synth) to weird (air-raid
siren). The repaired clay mouse sits on a bookshelf.
Clothes hang from a mounted stag's head in the corner.

Robin has set up camp in this room. It has the
atmosphere of a makeshift headquarters. A bolt hole in
a siege.

Tommy enters through a side door. He is nineteen, a
skinhead ex-squaddie. He is local. Deals speed in a
nearby pub. He has just woken up. He takes in the
unhinged door. He lets out a low whistle.

Robin Someone padlocked it.

Tommy Yeah. A guy came round.

37

Robin Who? What 'guy'?

Tommy The caretaker bloke who came round before.

Robin Greg? So he's jumped sides too? Goodo. Oliver must have bribed him.

He picks up the padlock and turns it in his hands.

It's like he's baiting me . . .

Over the scene he carefully re-hangs the door.

When did he come round?

Tommy This morning.

Robin While I was at the memorial? How elegant. I need a drink.

He goes to the bar.

Tommy You owe me some money.

Robin I'm aware of that, yes.

Robin What are you drinking?

Tommy Two hundred and forty quid.

Robin Let's have . . . gin.

He hands him a drink. Tommy doesn't take it, Robin sets it near him.

Cheers.

He raises his glass. Tommy doesn't drink.

(*His voice cracks.*) I've just been to my mother's memorial. Have one drink with me.

Beat.

Be a fucking human being for Christ's sake.

Tommy takes his drink.

Thank you.

They sip.

What's the time?

Tommy looks at the Pink Panther alarm clock.

Tommy One.

Robin Rats. I'm really late, aren't I? Sorry.

Tommy Yeah. You fucking are.

Robin I got waylaid in London you see. Plan A failed so I got stuck into Plan B. We outlined the plans, didn't we? Last night.

Tommy I don't remember.

He pulls back a bit of curtain to reveal details of Plan A, Plan B and Plan C scrawled on the wall.

Oh . . . yeah.

Robin Listen. Plan B. (*Reads from the wall.*) 'Going to every single person mother ever broke bread with to see if they will help me raise some pennies or dollar or moolah or fucking cash.' Moolah spelt pretty uniquely.

Beat.

Well, I did. After the memorial I went to everyone. Well, not everyone. A few people. The lawyer. That illustrator cunt.

Beat.

Turns out. When someone disappears into the middle of nowhere for years. People forget. People no longer . . . but it's OK. They couldn't evict me today or tomorrow. It would be too cruel. I call their bluff. You hear that? (*To the room.*) BLUFF!

Beat.

That was to the secret cameras Oliver probably . . . Or maybe to God. I don't know.

Tommy There are cameras?

Robin Unlikely. He's too tight for that.

Tommy Are you sure?

Robin Yes. I'm sure. Wow. What a day. You should have seen the crowd. Rotting monkeys in raincoats. Yacking away. Actually there was only about a dozen monkeys there. Hardly a crowd. Which was. Heartbreaking. Actually. I always thought . . .

Beat.

Anyway. Nobody I cornered seemed to be too keen to loan me the money. Which might have something to do with the fact I literally did actually definitely did corner them. So I rustled up a new plan.

Tommy What happened to A? You were keen on A.

Robin Ha. See. You do remember. Well. It would appear that taking out a mortgage to save this place is 'not a priority' for Oliver. Things got a bit heated after that. I think him and that girl are planning for a baby. She looked fatter then normal anyway. I know he had something to do with this. I know it. He convinced her to sell. He must have. I bet he handed her the bloody biro when she was out of her mind. She wouldn't have done this to me. She hasn't done this to me. Why you would bring a baby into this shit-hole of a planet I don't know. Have you been out there lately? Everyone is attached to a screen. It's the end of the fucking world, I'm convinced. No one. Looks at each other any more.

Beat.

It's sinister.

Beat.

But it's fine. I've got a new plan.

Tommy What happened to C?

Robin points at his black eye.

Robin Let's push the boat out and call the new one Plan D. D for . . . dastardly . . . D for . . .

Tommy Desperate.

Beat.

Robin Don't be a cunt. It doesn't suit you.

Tommy sets his empty drink down. Robin goes to refill it.

Tommy You said one drink.

Robin That was a half a drink. Look at the size of the glass.

He refills them both.

Robin I was born on this floor. Did you know that?

Tommy You mentioned it, yeah –

Robin Right there. Look at the stain. There. There on the floor.

Tommy About that two hundred and forty quid –

Robin How much more do you have on you? Last night. You said you had more.

Tommy I do, yeah.

Robin I'll buy all of it.

Tommy All of it?

Robin On one condition. You stay and do it with me.

Beat.

Come on. That's a win-win scenario if ever I heard one.

Tommy stares at him for a moment, then gets some wraps out of his sock. There are six in total.

Tommy I've got two gear, four MD.

Robin Done.

Tommy That makes it five-sixty then. In total.

Robin Wow. I'm going to have to go to a cashpoint for that. I'm imagining you don't take cheques.

Tommy Let's drive to one then.

Robin Yes. Little hiccup on that front.

Tommy Little what?

Robin I somewhat totalled the car in that tiny lane round the corner. So getting to a cashpoint this evening might be a bit tricky. I'll get the car towed tomorrow and we can get a lift into the village. You'll get your cash first thing I swear. Look. Here's my card. Keep it as collateral.

He offers him the card. Tommy doesn't take it. Robin ploughs on.

A Borrower couldn't drive down that lane. It's ridiculous. Although I suppose we are in mouse country . . . Little lanes for the talking, smoking, drink-driving mice –

Tommy What?

Robin It doesn't matter. Tomorrow. I swear. Cross my heart and hope to die.

He has racked up.

Line?

Tommy You should have told me you couldn't get the cash before you . . . What the fuck –

Robin Look. I'm sorry, but there isn't really another option. Unless you fancy a three-hour walk in the dark. I'll add interest.

Tommy How much?

Robin Let's call it a cool seven fifty. Look around you. I'm good for it. But only if you stay. I can't. I don't want to be on my own.

Tommy I don't know.

Robin does a line. Proffers the note to Tommy. He ignores it.

Robin I thought you were staying for a bit anyway. Like we agreed last night. We had a plan. We had several.

Tommy We were high.

Robin As a pilot's lunchbox, but that doesn't mean I didn't mean it, that means I didn't . . .

He tails off. He stares at his glass.

Mother's ruin.

Tommy What?

Robin That's what they call gin.

He jumps up.

Are you reneging? You are, aren't you? Don't fucking renegade.

Beat.

Please. You were going to stay. I was going to show you the lake and the woods and we were going to go shooting and I was going to lend you my crossbow and we were going to get high and drink what was left of the wine cellar then listen to jazz and shoot rabbits. It was going to be *ace*. It could still be *ace*. Why would you go back out there? Its just roads and shit pubs. There's a stag in our forest. A *stag* . . . Have you ever seen a real live stag before? Fucking stunning.

He goes to the window.

Come here. Look at the moon, the moonlight on the trees.

Beat.

When a view is that beautiful it's like God is flirting with you. Lifting his skirt, parting his legs.

Beat.

The slut.

He proffers the note again. After a beat Tommy takes it and walks over to do his line.

Tommy You could call a cab. For the cash. My phone's dead.

Robin No phone. And no signal.

Beat.

Phones and signal . . . Everyone is obsessed with fucking phones and fucking signals. In London at night, right. People walk around with their faces glowing like ghosts because they're all staring down at screens. It's fucking creepy.

Beat.

Have you been to London? I'd never been there till last year. Up till then I'd only been to the village and the town. Amazing when you think about it. London's like some futuristic film. Some apocalyptic . . . There are all these flashing lights. Everyone's just buying things. Selling and buying. Buying and selling. It's like we're just . . . eating everything up.

44

Beat.

If civilisation was a big fuck-off dinner party. No. A free buffet. We're right at the end gorging ourselves. It's the end of the world. And what's so weird is no one is acknowledging it. They're just . . . eating.

Beat.

Few weeks out here. Barefoot. When you go back, you see it for what it is. The end of our empire . . .

Pause.

Stay . . . just a night . . . Please . . . Have a fag at least. Look. I have tons.

He empties packets and packets on to the table. They are all different brands
    He comes close to Tommy and hands him one.

Robin One night.

Tommy You should ice that eye.

Robin We don't have any ice.

Tommy Let me see it.

Robin comes close. Tommy examines him. He holds his face for just a second to long. There is a flash of something. Tommy steps back. Robin stares at him. Right at him.
    Pause.

Robin You've got stains on your top you know.

Beat.

You can borrow one of mine.

Tommy takes his top off. On his back there is a St George's cross, large.

England.

Tommy I can't find one.

Robin Did you get that before or after you left service?

Tommy They're all filthy.

Robin You wouldn't tell me last night.

Tommy None of your business.

Robin I want to know. Which England is on your back? I want to know . . .

Tommy Do your drugs.

Robin Was it scary? Did you kill someone?

Tommy Leave it.

Robin Tell me.

Tommy Leave it, posh boy.

Robin I'm not posh.

Tommy Yeah. You're common, you.

Robin I'm sort of in the cracks. Home-schooled. Well, I sort of taught myself. We didn't have much money. This place. Ate it all really. First few years of my life we lived in this room, while she rebuilt the place. It was derelict until she. I suppose if I'm anything . . . I'm . . . I'm . . . landed gypsy . . .

Tommy You fucking are posh.

Robin Why?

Comes closer.

Do you want me to be?

Tommy stands his ground.
Pause. They stare at each other.
Tommy breaks the gaze first.

Robin Tell me why you left the army? I want to know.

Tommy Why did you?

Robin Leave? What? The academy?

Tommy The music place.

Robin I didn't like it. They wanted me to play things I didn't want to play. I didn't like the other students. I didn't like the way they . . . thought. I was educated with books, you see. I taught myself from pages. Actual physical pages. Not screens. I never went to real school. I never had a computer. So I didn't fit in. I wasn't native. I wasn't prepared for . . .

Tommy What?

Robin The internet. Technology. I was out here with the badgers and the books. I didn't even have phone. When I turned up everyone was fiddling with a mobile. I mean actually *everyone* in my class, as they waited for the induction to start, was staring onto a palm-sized screen. I counted.

Beat.

No one had told me, you see. No one had warned me. That this new mind was in session. That no one was present any more. That no one was actually. There. And this new mind, it turns out, is different. This new mind thinks in bursts. It trades information, not thoughts. It's post-post-post-Enlightenment. No one follows anything through. It's about knowledge, not thought. Knowledge over thought. And that's fucked up. That's wrong. Because knowing is not the same as thinking. We compare the two because knowing has more immediate value. And we fool ourselves that it is as useful but no one talks ideas anymore. Haven't you noticed? I noticed. Kids my age just trade information. And the future portends more and more information but no one is really thinking about it. Think about that . . .

Beat.

We're fucking up our minds. Maybe it takes an un-fucked mind to see it. Because without language, without proper narrative of thought, without the linear literary mind behind every intellectual revolution of the civilised world. What have we got left? We're marching into the dogs playing fucking Pacman on our phones. Brain cells . . . melting.

Pause.

Yikes. Good coke.

Pause.

Isn't it?

Although there was one thing I didn't mind about the new gizmos and gadgets.

Tommy And what's that?

Robin gestures to the synthesiser and sequencer.

Robin New music.

Tommy So that's why you left. Difference of –

Robin Philosophy. Yes. Well. That and . . . There was an incident.

Tommy Right.

Robin A fracas.

Tommy I see.

Robin You'd be amazed how far you can fit a phone in someone's mouth. If you really try.

Beat.

48

I tried to get a job afterwards but there was nothing.
They kicked me out of where I was living. Luckily I'd
made some friends. Twins. The boy-girl kind. I crashed
on their floor for a bit until. Well. Until.

Tommy You made friends?

Robin Don't act so surprised. But no. Not many other
students liked me if that's what you were getting at. Or
them for that matter. We formed a kind of splinter group.
They studied classical civilisation before music. We got on.

Pause. He looks right at Tommy.

You like me, though . . . don't you? We're friends,
wouldn't you say? Since we collided like nasty little stars
. . . Found me a soldier, didn't I? . . . It would be poetic if
we hadn't been bombing speed in the car park of the
Lamb and Cutlet. Or maybe that is poetic. I don't know.

Tommy You're all right.

They are close again. Robin stares at him.

Why are you looking at me like that?

Pause.

Robin (*quiet*) You know.

They hold each other's gaze.
Tommy breaks it.
Robin offers him the card again.

Keep it till tomorrow.

Tommy takes it.
Robin grins.

You're staying. Brilliant. Happy birthday to me. This is
going to be fun. I swear.

Tommy It's your birthday?

49

Robin Look, I even got a present. Oliver left it on my seat at the church. What do you reckon it is? A dismembered hand?

Now . . . as we've got drugs to do and a night to kill, shall we tuck into Plan D?

Tommy What's D involve then?

Robin Treasure.

Tommy Actual treasure?

Robin No. Babycakes. Not literally. The lawyer said, when I had him a little bit, a tiny bit, against a wall at the wake. Why people call these things wakes I do not know, it's not like she's fucking awake is it? Anyway, her lawyer said that maybe. Just maybe there were secret stocks, shares, something. He said she was a hoarder. Secretive like that. He didn't know. In fact he definitely doubted it. But I'm not in the business of doubt, I'm not in the business of daunt. So I reckon. If she hid anything. It's in there. (*Points at the birthday box.*) And I reckon there might just be something. Something to save the place. She wouldn't leave me without a lifeboat, right?

Tommy shrugs uneasily.

Long shot, yes, maybe, but. You have to look up. Don't you. Forward. Up. Never be daunted. Didn't Hemingway say that?

Tommy examines the birthday box.

Although he did shoot himself in the face. Is that being daunted? Or the opposite? I wonder . . .

Tommy It's locked.

Robin Yes. That's the thing. She always hid the key.

Tommy We don't need a key.

He picks up a hammer from the tool box.

Robin *No.* I don't want to break it.

Tommy regards him.

Tommy You're a strange one, you.

Robin Not unless I absolutely have to. Let's have a proper look for the key first. After these drinks. Cheers.

He raises his glass.

To treasure.

Tommy To treasure.

Beat.

I hate that thing.

He points at the stag's head.

It looks right at me I swear.

Robin Jesus? He's all right.

Robin pats him.

Tommy Dead things. Staring. Freaks me out.

Robin Ah. Then you're going to hate what we're having for dinner. Right. I'll check upstairs. You look in here. I might have missed it. A little gold key.

He exits.
Tommy lights a cigarette and pokes around the room half-heartedly. He opens the curtains, revealing three dead strung-up rabbits. He jumps.

Tommy Jesus.

He hears a car approaching. He whips the curtains closed.

ROBIN? ROBIN?

The crunch of gravel and voices.

There's someone here, ROBIN?

Footsteps.

Tommy jumps on to the makeshift bed and hides under the covers. Unknown to him his foot is poking out.

Arlo and Scout enter. They are twins, brother and sister, about the same age as Robin. They look distinctly alike. They are both still in their smart black memorial clothes. Scout has a black veil. Arlo carries a bottle of champagne and a bunch of slightly wilting flowers.

Scout ROBIN?

Tommy lies still.

Arlo Christ. Look at this place.

Arlo sniffs the air.

Cigarettes.

Scout See. He's definitely been back. I knew it, I told you –

Arlo No car though.

Scout Maybe he ditched it.

Arlo I hope so. He was too trashed to drive.

Scout Shhh . . .

Arlo What?

Scout Look, he's here . . .

Scout points to Tommy's visible foot.

Let's wake him.

They both creep towards Tommy and pounce on him.

Arlo / Scout HAPPY BIRTHDAY!

Tommy jumps up as they pounce. General physical confusion.

WHO THE FUCK ARE YOU?

Tommy I –

Arlo Get back, Scout.

Arlo grabs a fire poker.

He's a fucking burglar. Get your phone –

Tommy Wait –

Arlo NOW!

Tommy I'm a friend of Robin's –

Scout is fiddling with her phone.

Arlo Scout, what the hell are you –

Scout There's no signal.

Arlo Stand on something.

Scout What?

Arlo For a signal. Stand on something. Wave it around. WAVE THE PHONE AROUND.

She stands on the table. She waves her phone around.

Scout Do I dial the local police or nine-nine-nine?

Arlo Nine-nine-nine.

Tommy I can describe him. Skinny. Twenties. Suit. Black eye. We met in the pub last night. Look. There's his top.

Tommy picks up Robin's suit jacket and throws it at Arlo.

See!

Arlo Look at it, Scout.

Scout I thought you told me to get back, you big man, you.

Arlo Fucking look at it.

She does.

Scout It's his.

Arlo doesn't lower his poker.

Tommy You can ask him yourself. ROBIN!

Arlo Even so. I think you should go.

Scout Arlo . . .

Arlo What? He's some random guy Robin picked up when he was hammered, he shouldn't still be here. Either that or he's a burglar. He needs to leave.

Tommy I don't think that's up to you.

Arlo Look, mate –

Tommy My name is Tommy.

Arlo Look, Tom –

Tommy Tommy.

Arlo Whatever. Our friend is very fragile at the moment and prone to making rash decisions. Today is his birthday and we've come down to see him. I'm sure you've had a nice time but I think things would be a lot simpler if you went on your way. It's getting late now. Time to go. All right?

Tommy just stares at him.

All right?

Tommy keeps staring.

Put it this way. If you don't go I'll call the police.

Tommy's eyes flicker.

Ha. Knew it. You don't like that so much, do you? I know your type. He's picked people up like you before. Now fuck off.

Tommy What do you mean, people like me?

Arlo Well. You're hardly a fucking florist.

Tommy If you call the police. I'll be forced to tell them. What I sold him.

Arlo We'll cross that rainbow when we come to it.

Scout He's got a point.

Arlo No he doesn't.

Scout Robin will freak out if you call. It'll be awful. Like last time, remember –

Arlo That crackhead rent boy robbed him, we had to –

Scout But they gave Robin a caution too –

Arlo Give me the phone.

There is the sound of a tile falling off the roof.

What was . . .

> *Another.*
> *Scout goes outside.*

Scout Oh my God.

Arlo What?

Scout He's on the roof. Robin's on the fucking roof.

Arlo WHAT?

> *They exit.*
> *There is a sudden sickening crash. Scout screams.*
> *Tommy rushes outside.*
> *Arlo and Tommy carry Robin in. He is covered in*
> *leaves and dirt and holding a home-made flag. They*
> *lay him on the sofa.*

Arlo Is he unconscious? What do we do?

Scout Pour water over him, or is that when someone faints –

Arlo Maybe I should slap him. Oh God –

Tommy Get away –

Arlo Leave him –

Tommy Just calm down.

Tommy very expertly puts Robin in the recovery position. Robin opens his eyes

Robin What happened?

Arlo Thank God.

Robin sits up.

You fell off the roof. That's what happened.

Robin's face cracks into a smile.

Robin You're *here*! You're both here. You came. To help. Of course you did. Come here.

He embraces both the twins at once. They tangle into a pile. They seem to forget Tommy is there. He watches. Uneasy.

Arlo What were you doing, you idiot? You scared us.

Robin I wanted to put the flag up. I found it in the attic. She always did it on my birthday, so I –

Scout If that tree hadn't been there you could have –

Scout – broken your neck.

Robin Shhh.

Scout It was horrible.

They nuzzle together.

Robin Shhh . . . I'm a miracle. A solid-gold baby.

Scout and Robin kiss. On the mouth. Arlo remains tangled between them. Tommy stands awkwardly.

Arlo I saw what happened after the service.

Robin A difference of opinion, that's all.

Arlo What happened to your eye? Oliver didn't –

Robin Oliver wouldn't have the balls. I'm so happy you're here . . .

He sits up suddenly.

Hold on. He didn't send you, did he?

Arlo / Scout Of course not.

Robin Promise?

Arlo Swear.

Robin Champagne. Brillo. Lets make cocktails. Let's have a toast.

Scout You're bleeding. We should wash that –

Robin Then cocktails?

Scout Exactly.

She exits leading Robin by the hand. Arlo and Scout share a look behind Robin's back.
Tommy waits a moment then turns to Arlo.

Tommy Are they . . .

Arlo What?

Tommy Together?

Arlo Yes. No. I don't know. Sometimes.

Arlo notices the stack of instruments.

Has he been playing?

Tommy He played last night.

Arlo Well, that's good. At least.

He examines the stack.

Arlo Quite a selection. Is that an . . . air-raid siren? I don't think we're going to get much of this in the car. Oh well. We can send a taxi back I suppose.

Arlo starts gathering some of Robin's things.

Tommy What are you doing?

Arlo Taking him home. Obviously.

Tommy I don't think he'll like that.

Arlo You've known him all of twenty-four hours, Man Friday. I don't think your opinion is –

Tommy I'm serious. I don't think –

Arlo Forgive me. But I don't give a fuck what you think.

Beat.

Oops. Sorry. Did I say that out loud?

Tommy I'm telling him what you're doing.

Tommy heads to the kitchen door. Arlo darts ahead and closes it quietly.

Arlo For Christ's sake listen to me. Robin is not meant to be here. At all. Contracts complete first thing tomorrow morning. Or did he not tell you that during your little . . . midnight feast? He didn't, did he? Look. If he's not gone by tomorrow there will be an almighty shit storm. Oliver's held the developers off for as long as possible. The press are already sniffing around the story. First her suicide. Then that fracas at the memorial. He needs to leave. This . . . protest . . . has gone on long enough. I mean, look at this place. It's bloody freezing. And the smell . . . Christ. I can hardly believe it's the same house.

Beat.

Look. It will really help us if you go. We're much more likely to convince him to leave. And trust me that's the best thing for him. I'll give you a lift to the station.

Tommy I'm not going unless he wants me to.

Arlo How much is he paying you to stay with him?

Beat.

Arlo He is, isn't he? I knew it.

Tommy I'm helping him fix the place up.

Arlo What place? There is no place, don't you get it? This house is gone. Sold. Tonight is his last night here.

Tommy Why should I believe you?

Arlo Why would I lie?

Tommy How did you get in the gate? If the numbers were changed?

Arlo He's paying you. How pathetic, make money another way, this is ridiculous.

Tommy Don't avoid the –

Arlo You're a drug dealer. Go and lurk somewhere –

Tommy How do you know I'm just a drug dealer?

Arlo Well what are you then? A nanny? A rent boy? A florist? What?

Tommy Stop saying florist, why do you keep saying florist?

Arlo I LIKE THE WAY IT SOUNDS.

Small pause.

Look. Mate.

Tommy I am not your mate.

Arlo Tommy. Look. Listen. Please. Let's start again. How much does he owe you?

Tommy None of your business.

Arlo This is my business. He is my business, you idiot. And right now, I'm trying, whether you believe it or not, to help him. He doesn't want to be here tomorrow when they come. He just doesn't.

Beat.

I doubt he has a dime, you know. You're better getting the money off me. How much?

Tommy I don't want your money.

Arlo Only his. It's all the same. you know. Look. I'll pay you, right now.

Tommy doesn't move.

Then it isn't just about money, is it?

Beat.

Shit. My ears just pricked . . . they just blushed . . . Ooo la la, Man Friday. Have you got a crush?

Tommy steps threateningly close. Arlo backs away grinning.

Arlo I wouldn't get too carried away with it if I were you. He has this effect on people sometimes. He's so very. Himself. So very. Untouched. That he makes you feel. Well . . . how to put it . . . awake . . . doesn't he?

Tommy Look, 'mate'. I don't like you. I didn't from the moment you ponced in that door. I am staying put simply because I don't believe a word that comes out of your sordid little mouth. Robin says he'll pay me tomorrow

and I believe him. I want no part in your . . . dirty little . . .
Disneyland. So shut. The. Fuck. Up.

Arlo You know what, the first time I think I fully
understood Robin he was sitting on a ledge high up
Tower Bridge. He'd climbed the metal suspension bit
with a keyboard slung across his back. And he was sat
there. About fifty feet above the Thames. Sat there playing.
Just to himself. And when he was asked why, he answered,
'Why not? It has the best view.'

Tommy What's your fucking point?

Arlo Someone must have called the police because they
turned up and try to get Robin down. At first they were
nice to him, it looked a bit like a suicide bid, I suppose.
But pretty quickly they started getting angry because it
became obvious he wasn't only far from suicidal but
having a top-dollar time and had no plans to come down.

  Beat.

They start shouting but Robin doesn't understand, you
see. He isn't opposing traffic, he isn't bothering anyone.
Why can't he stay there? They say that it's against the
law. Whose law, Robin says? They've got a megaphone
now but Robin just ignores them and turns around to
keep on playing. More police come. And now people are
starting to gather. To watch. The sun is high above the
river and the buildings glint. London looks like Gotham.
The horizon like . . . teeth. And there he is, sat on his
ledge like a monkey in a tree, like a pig in shit. His grin
was . . . enormous.

  Beat.

This is getting embarrassing for the police now, you
understand. The crowd are on Robin's side and it's
getting a bit tense. The Fire Brigade arrives and start
unwinding a bungee-type thing. They harness up their

sportiest-looking fireman and you can see that their plan is to lower their guy over to Robin. Harness him up and get to safety.

Beat.

So after a whole load of palaver with the equipment, sporty fireman gets dangled off the side of the bridge until he's hanging above Robin. He reaches out to grab him but Robin bends out of his reach, keeps playing. Sporty fireman is pissed off now so decides to use all his weight and push himself off the side of the bridge in a final attempt to swing down and grab at our scoundrel Robin. This looks like it's going to work. As he swings the crowd takes a collective breath, but just before he can reach out and touch him . . . Robin . . . jumps.

Beat.

With nothing to grab hold of, the fireman swings back and collides hard with the side of the bridge. There was this horrible crack. The crack of the bone on wrought iron. The fireman screams as Robin surfaces. Grinning in the Thames. Slick as an otter. Smug as a cat.

Beat.

You can see it on YouTube

Tommy What's your point?

Arlo My point is. It's easy to think Robin is romantic. Free. Blah blah blah. But actually he's ruthless. He's always looking for the best view. At whatever. Cost.

Tommy What do you mean?

Arlo I don't think he has the money he promised you. I'd bet my life on it.

Tommy He can tell me that himself.

Arlo Wow. Bitten hard, aren't you? It's almost sweet.

Tommy You have no idea what you're fucking talking about.

Arlo Oh, I think I do.

Tommy I am going to let what you said go, only, and listen to this, *only*, because I like your friend and I don't want any trouble. I am going to stay here until *he* tells me to go and *he* sorts out his debt, because I need the money, but I am not going to take orders from some jumped-up Little Lord Fuckweasel . . .

Arlo Instead you'll be paid by one. Like a servant. How revolutionary . . .

Robin and Scout re-enter with tea.

Robin Tea. Marvellous, isn't it? I feel reborn. And look what I found! It was in the teapot.

Robin brandishes the key. He notices Arlo's attempt at packing.

What are you doing? Are you packing? Is he packing for me?

Arlo Swallows and Amazons are over, Robin. It's time to go.

Robin I thought you came here to help.

Arlo Some day. Soon. You'll understand that this is –

Scout Helping. You can sleep in the car.

Robin Put that down. Am I your child?

Arlo No –

Robin Am I your brother? Your sister? Your –

Scout We're your best friends

Robin Exactly. So respect my wishes and –

Arlo You can't stay here with him. Are you insane? Look at you.

Robin If I stick to my half of the house I can do what I damn well want. I'm staying here to write music and fix the roof. I'm staying here to make things because making –

Arlo Robin. They complete tomorrow.

Robin What?

Arlo I spoke to your lawyer after the service. You were hardly talking to me. I. We. Wanted to find out what was going on –

Robin Tomorrow?

Arlo I think you knew that. Didn't you . . .

Pause.

Robin I was born here. My mother restored this house. She built it back up from the ruin it was with her bare fucking hands. I woke up to the sound of hammers that sounded like drums and guns for the first three years of my life. This is our land. No printed words and no paper can change that. No money. Which is, by the way, *only fucking paper*, can change that.

Pause.

Arlo I know you're upset. I know this is hard. I know how much this place means to you, Robin. But life will go on. Money from the sale can set you up somewhere again. Give you some time to grieve, some time to write, a place of your own, it's not to be sniffed at –

Robin There isn't any money. She remortgaged again and again to keep building it. It's not about that. It's not about FUCKING MONEY. Why is EVERYTHING? About fucking MONEY? I saw these people, in London, who slept on the streets, who asked people who walked past, for money. And even though they had money and the person on the floor didn't, they would just ignore them. Like they weren't there. Like they didn't exist. Money is *fucked*. We have no concept of what it costs us.

He is agitated, his breathing jagged.

Once I saw a man walk out of a shop in London and piss himself and start crying. In the street. In the day. And no one did *a thing*. He'd pissed himself and his face was all twisted and he was there in the middle of the street and no one. No one –

Scout Calm down, baby.

Robin 'Calm down'? Everyone's gone mad. Mad. And it's me that should calm down? We could have made anything and we made that? That place? Mad. Out there it's *mad*. The ship is on fire and I feel like it's only me who can see it. You're just used to it, don't you get that? You're fucking *blind*. I'm staying here. Where there's animals, where there's light.

He kneels in front of the birthday box.

Scout What are you doing? I think he's about to be sick –

Robin opens the box.
    He pours the contents on to the floor. There are several boxes of fireworks and some costumes. He roots through it. Nothing. Silence. He looks up at Tommy. Their eyes meet.

What were you looking for?

Robin It doesn't matter.

Pause.

I used to defend this place you know. When I was little. She'd send me down to the gate to tell people to go away. I had a spear and everything Well. It was a stick. A really pointy stick.

Robin seems about to cry.

Arlo Sometimes being brave is knowing when to give up, Robin.

Robin Oh do fuck off, Arlo.

Robin hangs his head. They watch him for a moment. He composes himself and looks up.

How did you get in the gate?

Arlo The code.

Robin The numbers you used before? In the summer? How did you remember it?

Arlo I saved it on my phone –

Scout We could stay here tonight if you want? To say goodbye.

Arlo Scout. I don't think that's a good –

Scout It's his family home, Arlo. Give him a few hours –

Arlo Is that what you want?

Robin nods.

Then you'll come? Back in the car with us? Promise?

Robin nods.

Arlo Fine. But we need to leave early.

Scout What do you want to do?

Robin I don't know.

Scout We could make dinner. We can do whatever you want. It's still your birthday.

Robin My birthday. Yes.

Scout What did she do on your birthday, how did you do it here?

Robin Costumes. Fireworks. A party.

Scout OK, let's have one. Let's have a little party.

Robin Like they did on the *Titanic*.

Scout Exactly. Go down . . . dancing.

She picks up the costumes. She holds up the Cleopatra.

Was this hers?

Robin nods. He gets up to make drinks. He makes a punch out of the champagne and dashes of other spirits. He has his back to the others. Unknown to them he pours the powder into the punch. He uses four of the wraps.

Sexy.

Robin She was, actually.

Arlo Those are amazing, so detailed.

Scout holds up the Cleopatra mask. Robin stares at it for a moment then hands out the drinks. There is some left in the jug. He puts it on the side. He never actually drinks in this scene.

Scout Come on then. Let's dress up.

Tommy Why?

Scout Why not?

She hands out costumes. They get dressed. The costumes are a mixture of courtly and animal. A Prince for Robin, Knight for Arlo, Ophelia for Scout and the last, a jester, is left for Tommy. Animal tails

67

*and ears are added at random. There are capes and fur.
The costumes should be a twist on the traditional. A
nightmare pantomime.*

   *Arlo goes to turn on some music. The same song
Lily played in Act One comes on. Robin startles. He
snaps it off. He swops it for something else.*

Tommy I don't know about this –

Arlo Aw . . . you shy?

Tommy This isn't really my thing.

Robin It's the only thing that will fit you. Come on. It'll
be fun.

Arlo It's a party. Put it on.

Tommy You must have something else.

Arlo If you're staying you're playing.

Robin As a birthday present. Please.

Arlo Didn't realise you were vain.

Tommy Fuck off.

   He snatches the costume.

Happy birthday.

Arlo Amazing . . .

   *Robin has picked up the Cleopatra costume. He drops
it as if it is on fire. He stares at it on the floor. Scout
watches him.*

Scout Robin?

   Robin shoves it away

Tommy Now what? Do we just sit around in them?

Arlo God, you're a fucking laugh, aren't you?

Robin Let's play hide-and-seek.

Tommy Seriously?

Scout That could be fun.

Arlo I'm up for it.

Tommy OK . . .

Robin I'm going to close my eyes and count to ten. Right. But first things first. Down it.

They down the drinks.

Right. Hide.

He puts on Lily's mask.

One . . . two . . .

Scout runs off outside, Tommy and Arlo both try and hide behind the curtain. The dead rabbits are revealed. Arlo jumps. Tommy recoils. Arlo spots his weakness and waves one of the carcasses at Tommy. Tommy darts out of the kitchen doors. Arlo wins and gets to stay behind the curtain.

Robin opens his eyes. He listens for a moment, then, satisfied that no one is there, he goes to the dressing-up box and pulls out the Cleopatra dress. He takes it to the sofa and sits down; he buries his face in it. He rocks back and forth. He twists it in his hands.

Arlo peers out from the curtains. He watches Robin, who doesn't notice. Arlo creeps out.

Arlo Robin . . .

Robin Jesus. You scared me.

He pulls off the mask.

Arlo Do you want to . . . We don't have to . . . We could just –

Robin You're shit at hide-and-seek. OUT!

Arlo I'm worried about you –

Robin I told you. I'm fine.

Regards him.

Arlo Bullshit.

Robin Death can make you feel more alive, you know. And I do. I feel . . . I've been making things. Making music. I've been building things. It's the opposite of dying, making things, isn't it –

Arlo I suppose.

Beat.

Look at me.

Robin does.

Tell me the truth.

Robin There isn't a word.

Arlo Try one.

Robin If there was a word. And there isn't. It would be a word so . . . terrible. A word so . . . frightening. That it would have to be kept in a box. And never taken out. It would be a word so . . . dangerous. That your mouth would break as you tried to make the sound.

Arlo Oh Robin.

Robin Nobody tells you what you'll think. About bodies. About flesh.

Pause.
He leans in to Arlo. Their foreheads touch. Arlo hugs him. Clumsily they begin to kiss. It is aching. Real. Scout appears in the window. She sees. Robin pulls away

Robin I can't do this.

Arlo You want to. You fucking want to.

They kiss again.

I've been so scared that this was my fault. You ran away after we kissed last time. Came here. Got drunk and then she –

Robin It wasn't your fault.

Robin breaks away. He backs away.

Arlo Robin. Don't. Don't run away. Don't –

Robin exits.

ROBIN!
  Fuck.

*He gets out his phone. He dials and goes outside.
    Tommy enters and takes off his costume. Scout
appears in the garden doors and watches him.*

Scout Not hiding either?

He ignores her.

That's a big tattoo.
  My brother's a twat. I know that. I'm sorry.

Nothing.

I've got a tattoo. Look.

*She shows him her ankle. There is a wing crudely
tattooed on the side.*

Tommy Who did that? It looks –

Scout Home-made? Arlo did it. He's got one too. A wing each. It really hurt. Really really hurt.

Tommy Why'd you let him do it? If it hurt?

Scout We used to play games. Away at school together. Dares, really. I dared him to run into the road once. I didn't think he would do it. He broke his arm. In exchange, he was allowed to tattoo me. With a needle and a biro. It took hours. We did it in an empty classroom. Now whenever I'm in pain I smell chalk.

Tommy Why a wing?

Scout So . . . It's really stupid actually. He was obsessed with Hermes. Its so together we can fly.

Tommy Are you fucking him?

Scout Arlo?

Tommy Robin. Are you . . .
  There's just a bit of an atmosphere. I wondered.

Scout I see –

Tommy A bit of a vibe.

Scout I get it.

Tommy Well?

Scout How old are you?

Tommy Twenty-two.

  Beat.

Scout You look younger. Why are you really here?

Tommy Money.

Scout I don't believe that's the only reason.

Tommy It's a pretty big fucking reason if you're me. I'm not one of you.

Scout What do you mean, 'one of us'? We're all people. We're all humans. We all shit. We all stink.

Tommy But some of us shit in the woods. If you know what I mean.

Scout Yes. Because Arlo and I are basically shitting on silken clouds.

Tommy I wouldn't be surprised.

Scout Well, Robin definitely shits in the woods occasionally, so your argument's bust. Anyway. We digress. I was apologising for my brother.

Tommy Thank you.

She takes him in.

Scout You have a nice face.

Scout looks at her hands. She flexes them.

I'm. I'm getting traces. Weird.

Pause.

Do you feel a little . . . ?

Tommy What?

Scout Weird. Tingly.

She sits.

I must be tired or something. Low blood sugar maybe. I haven't eaten in a while. Wasn't really the day for it.

She leans her head on his shoulder. Tommy sits stiffly. Surprised.

It used to be so nice here, you know. Nicer than anywhere I had ever been. I only visited once but it was magic. We had a tea party for her birthday. Robin put flowers in her hair. They seemed. Very in love. Is that weird? To say that? But that is how it seemed. Fucked-up definitely. But . . . sort of incredible . . . and now she's dead. Oh well. Hey-ho.

73

Tommy smells her hair. She notices.

Did you just . . . smell my hair?

Tommy No.

She sits up straight.

Scout Hilarious.

Arlo enters, brushing leaves off himself.

Arlo Good. You're both here.

He closes the doors and lowers his voice.

I spoke to Oliver. I had to climb a fucking tree to get a signal but I got through.

Beat.

Hold on. Why are you sitting together?

Scout Why? Does it bother you?

Arlo No, it's just a bit . . .

Scout drapes herself around Tommy.

Scout Uncomfortable for you?

Arlo What's going on?

She slides on to Tommy's lap. He looks terrified.

Scout Because I wouldn't want to make you uncomfortable, darling twin. I wouldn't tread that line.

Arlo Mankoi, Scout –

Scout Intya toror –

Scout – sut mankoi I mela ho delotha Ila delotha Ila –

Arlo – I mela ho vithell –

Scout – ro haba dhaeraow –

Arlo – I mela ho vithell –

74

Tommy What the fuck? You sound mad.

Scout A third of the English dictionary was made up
by a –

Arlo / Scout – madman, don't you know.

Scout Alye then.

Arlo Alye.

They touch hands briefly.

Anyway, quick, before he. Look, I've got an offer for
you.

Scout For me?

Arlo No. For Man Friday. To help us get him in the car
tomorrow. Just in case he pulls any funny business. I told
him we were staying here tonight and he suggested. You're
stronger than us and. I think between you and me –

Tommy So the brother did send you. I knew it.

Arlo Don't you get it? He's been lying to you. He doesn't
have a fucking dime. I suspected as much but Oliver is
certain.

He starts writing a out a cheque.

He had to borrow twenty quid off the lawyer for petrol.
Oliver says he'll cover Robin's debt to you if you help us.
And he'll throw in a grand more. As a thank you for
helping during, I quote, 'a difficult time'.

Tommy Judas.

Arlo You said you needed the money. Really needed it.

Tommy just stares.

You'll see. He doesn't have a penny. This is a serious offer.
Just to help. That's all. It's the right thing for him. And you
do. Seem to care.

He shows Tommy the cheque.

Look . . . I'm putting it in my pocket. Think about it.

Scout is staring at her hands, flexing them.

Scout?

Scout Think I need some air.

Scout goes out the garden doors.
   Arlo stares hard at Tommy.

Arlo And by the way. Don't even think about it.

Scout suddenly reappears. She is ashen.

Scout I . . . I . . . There's a . . . I can see . . . It looks like –

Arlo See what?

Scout There's the shadow. A moving shadow, of a woman, an hooded woman . . .

Arlo Don't be ridiculous.

Scout Look.

He sticks his head around the door.

OK. Right. Yes. There is a silhouette. Coming up the drive. Getting closer. Yes. Right. That's definitely happening.

Tommy You're winding me . . .

He looks. Yelps, turns to the others open-mouthed.
   There is the sound of footsteps. Crunching gravel.

Arlo Oh shit oh shit oh shit.

Esme (*off*) ROBIN?

Arlo Oh God oh God oh God.

All three hide behind the sofa. Huddling close together.

76

Esme ROBIN?

The door opens. Tommy, Arlo and Scout cower. Esme is revealed. A girl of Robin's age. She is in a hooded raincoat and holding an oil lantern. From a distance she would have looked eerie and frightening.

Hello? Robin?

She walks around the side of the sofa and sees the others. They all have their eyes closed and are holding hands.

Esme Hi.

Arlo opens his eyes.

Arlo It's Sarah! Thank God. Living breathing one-hundred-per-cent real. Sarah. Come here.

Arlo clasps her. She clearly hates it. He releases her.

Esme (*icy*) Scout.

Scout (*equally icy*) Esme.

Arlo Who's Esme?

Esme My. Name. Is. Esme.

Arlo Shit. Sorry. Esme. Of course. It's OK. We're OK! Esme, we're OK. Fucking hell. That was trippy.

Esme What is he talking about? Where is Robin? Who is that boy? And what the hell has happened to this room?

Arlo We thought you were a ghost, Robin's wandered off, that's Tommy, he's a florist, and . . . Robin's squatted the room.

Esme It's freezing in here.

She turns on the portable heater.

Tommy Who are you?

Esme Sarah. Apparently.

Scout She's Robin's . . . cousin?

Esme Childhood friend. Actually. Do you two listen to anything that isn't completely . . . Never mind. Where is he?

No one answers. They look a bit disoriented.

Esme For fuck's sake wake up. Where is he?

Arlo We were playing hide-and-seek. I think he's still. Hiding.

Esme Shall someone have a little look for him, maybe? You know, given the circumstances.

Small pause. Tommy nods and exits.

Thank you.

She starts to tidy the room as best she can.

Esme How is he?

Arlo OK. Ish. I suppose.

Esme He was in such a state at the memorial.

Scout You were there?

Esme Of course I was there. I should have been here earlier. Dad was so distressed after the service. It took me a while to get him back home and into bed. Jesus. Look at this place. What's that smell?

Scout I saw a man crying. The only one.

Esme Well, that was him. It really upset him to see Robin that far . . . gone.

She stops tidying and sighs.

God . . . Look at this place. It used to be so. She used to be so . . . I need a drink.

She goes to the spiked jug and pours a large glass.
Throughout the scene she drinks it.

Scout How did he know her?

Esme He taught Robin piano. Until they went . . .
completely underground. Has he eaten anything?

Scout There's some . . . some . . . rabbits.

Despite herself she starts to laugh.

Esme Do you think this is funny?

Scout Pardon? No. It's just been a weird day –

Esme Do you think what's happened here is funny, that
it's a game?

Arlo No. Obviously we don't.

Esme Then why the hell are you tittering behind a sofa,
high on drugs? You're having a grand old time, aren't
you? This is just another party.

Beat.

I don't think you realise.

Beat.

This is just tourism for you.

Arlo Now look here. We are most certainly not high on
drugs. How dare you suggest that we would take
advantage –

Esme Have you seen your faces?

Scout We came here to get him. This is a party, he
wanted a party. He's leaving. Tomorrow. He's coming
home.

Esme Back with you? Home with you?

79

Scout Yes.

Esme He was fine before he met you, you know. A bit weird. But fine. You . . .

Scout What? Corrupted him? He's a big boy, Esme.

Esme You have no clue, do you?

Scout Do you not think he maybe changed because he left home and his mother got sick? That his life changed. That maybe, just maybe, it wasn't evil old us.

Esme No. I don't actually.

Scout I think you're just angry that . . .

Esme That what?

Scout He outgrew you.

Esme smiles slowly.

Esme You think what you do and how you act is grown-up? Do you think that being rich and being from the city and being talented makes you better? If you actually were so happy with yourselves you'd stop following Robin around like dogs. You know you're a bit crap, don't you? A bit unjustified . . . That's why you need him around. Because for some reason. He validates you.

Arlo Bitch.

Esme What you don't seem to understand, because you're too busy pretending you're in some sexy little film of your own lives, is what you think is exciting about him is actually damage.

Scout That's not what we –

Esme He was kept here, Scout. Away from everything. He barely went to the village. He grew up in his own weird little kingdom shooting things and wearing no shoes. Half the reason he's excellent at the piano is there was quite literally, nothing. Else. To. Do. She wouldn't let him go to school. Do you ever wonder why he talks like Peter Pan on crack? All that yikes, crikey, rats vernacular. That's because his only friends as a kid were his mother and a battered Enid Blyton. He actually thought that's how people talked. No wonder he went crazy when she finally felt guilty enough to encourage him to leave. He'd never been to London. He barely knew anyone his own age. He was sent there totally unarmed. He was, in his own way . . . innocent.

Beat.

If you really care about him. Leave him alone after this. He needs to find his own way now. He doesn't need to be. Encouraged.

Beat.
   Scout gets out a compact mirror and looks at her own eyes.

Scout Um. My pupils are huge, They look like they could eat me.

Blinks.

Eat me.

Arlo holds her face. They stare at each other. It dawns on them.

Arlo Oh my God.

Tommy appears in the doorway.

Tommy I can't find him.

Arlo You. What did you give us? What did you fucking give us?

Tommy I think Robin may have . . . I think maybe he . . .

He points to Esme's empty glass.

Esme Did I drink the drugs?

Beat.

I drank the drugs.

Arlo starts laughing.

This is NOT funny.

Arlo It really is.

Tommy finds the empty wraps on the bar.

Tommy Wow. It was all of the MDMA.

Arlo How much?

Tommy Four grams.

Arlo whistles.

Esme What's going to happen to me?

Scout You're going to be fine.

Esme I get fucking drug tested. Fuck. Fuck. Fuck.

Tommy What do you do?

Esme I'm training to be a policewoman.

Arlo Now that really is funny.

Esme FUCK OFF!

Scout It's OK. I promise. If you relax you'll feel good.

Esme I don't want to feel good. I want to feel fucking normal. I'll lose my job.

Arlo A policeman. Seriously?

Esme Policewoman.

Arlo Wow. A real life policewoman.

Esme DO YOU HAVE ANY IDEA HOW HARD IT IS TO GET A JOB AT THE MOMENT? ANY IDEA?

Arlo Wow. Relax.

Esme DO NOT TELL ME TO RELAX, YOU UTTER COCK.

Scout This will be out of your system in a week. Take time off.

Esme It doesn't work like that. What planet are you guys on? Fuck. Fuck.

Arlo The same planet you're going to be on in a minute.

Esme IT'S NOT FUCKING FUNNY.

She reigns herself in. Tries to compose herself. She wins. Just. But is shaky.

Mind over matter. Mind over matter.

Scout I won't leave your side, OK? I promise it will be fine. But you've got to go with it. Ride it.

They sit together. Close. Scout takes her hand.

Esme Will I see things?

Scout Unlikely.

Arlo I see things on MDMA sometimes.

Scout SHUT. UP. Arlo.

Tommy Maybe you should make yourself sick.

Esme I feel tingly.

Scout A good tingle though, right? Make it a good tingle.

Arlo If she's sick it'll still be in her system and she won't get the high.

Tommy I don't think she wants the high –

Arlo Well, she might as well embrace it now.

Suddenly the lights cut.

Scout What's going on –

Arlo The power, it must have –

Tommy There's a fuse box over –

Suddenly there is the sound of piano playing. It is classical. Rachmaninov. Perfectly executed.

Scout Robin?

Arlo Robin, that's fucking creepy.

A few more notes.

Robin Thing is.

Beat.

It wasn't that I couldn't play what they wanted. I could do it with my eyes shut.

Esme ROBIN, STOP IT!

Scout You've spiked us, haven't you?

Robin I could say no but that would be lying, but then again you know all about lying don't you . . .
Rosencrantz and Guildenstern are . . .

Beat.

Fucked.

A bright torch snaps on. Robin aims it at each of them.

Robin The code for the gate was changed. Oliver changed it. He must have given you the new numbers. That's the only way you could have got in.

Beat.

Robin You lied.

Scout It was for you. To help you

Robin What did he offer you? Money. What?
  Is that Esme? You've been sent too? Who do you have to fuck for some loyalty around here? Christ.

Esme I have nothing to do with this.

Robin I don't believe you.

Esme I climbed the gate by the woods, I came here on foot. I haven't spoken to Oliver. I wouldn't know how to even call him. You know that.

Robin You of all people –

Scout She's telling the truth.

Arlo OK, look, Robin, we spoke to him, but it wasn't for anything, we're not profiting from this I swear, we wanted to help, we're here for you, we *are*.

Robin Liar liar.

Scout It's true.

Robin Breeches on fire . . .

He stares at them.
  Coby appears in the doorway.

Angel.

Coby I saw the lights, then none, then one came on again.

Robin My angel, my mouse, she followed the light, come here.

Robin puts his arm around her, she clings to him.

Coby Happy birthday.

Robin You're just in time. Look at them. Look at you. Monkeys in my headlights. Woke up you up a bit, that. Didn't it. Got you back in the room. Into the *present*. Is that much to ask? To be in the very second you actually exist in. Animals are. And we're animals. Or we're meant to be.

Arlo Robin. Please. Let's just. Why don't we sit down –

Robin Every fucking fibre of me is alive in this moment, my body aches and my head shrieks and you're telling me to sit down, you're telling me to . . . maybe you should STAND UP.

Beat.

Think of everything in the world that is going on this very second. The noses being blown. The toast being burnt. The plates being dropped. The wheels screeching, wings beating, mouths screaming. The sun setting and falling and setting and falling. The babies born, the guns shot, the waves crashing.

All. Right. Now. Can't you feel it? If you try you *can.*

Beat.

You've seen someone die, Tommy. I can tell. You've got that glint in your eye. Light on metal. Doesn't it make everything seem possible? Doesn't it make you. In the strangest way. Free.

Tommy nods.

Robin There are heartbeats everywhere. Hear them. *Everywhere.* Let's celebrate.

Robin switches on a dance track by remote. He goes to the piano and plays along as the song builds and builds.

Dance or something. Go on. In Mexico they dance for the dead. They celebrate. *Do it.* They do it. They dance, they *celebrate.*

He whips his arms into the air.

Fucking DANCE!

They all dance. Arlo and Scout join in with making the music. They grab instruments and the sequencer. They riff off Robin's piano, then off each other, building the song into a ferocious climax.

Robin lets them take over and gets out cans of paint. He opens one and in a sudden movement throws the contents. Colour slashes across the wall. He gives everyone a can. One by one in wild abandon they join him. The paint fight is chaos. Joyful. Anarchic.

Slowly Robin becomes still amidst the pandemonium. They don't notice. He unwraps his present. It is a metronome. He places it on top of the piano.

He takes the fireworks and slips out of the garden door. The paint fight continues. Esme has stopped fighting and is dancing wildly in the corner. Only Coby notices Robin is missing.

Coby Where did –

Esme is still dancing to a beat in her head.

Esme Dance like this, guys, like this.

She is trying to get them to follow a synchronised dance. Scout tries to copy her.

Yes, Scout.

Scout Whoop whoop.

Esme Yes, Scout.

Scout Whoop.

Arlo joins in. Tommy is bent over laughing.

Coby GUYS.

They all turn.

Where's –

There is a bang. The sky outside flashes. Tommy ducks down as if for cover.

It's only a firework.

They go to the garden doors. Another bang. Robin is setting off the fireworks.
Tommy flinches at every bang. Cowers.

She used to do it every year on his birthday.

Arlo He's doing it a bit close to the –

Tommy Has he put it –

Another bang.

Holy shit –

BANG BANG BANG.

Scout The barn . . . It's on fire.

They charge outside.
After a moment Robin creeps in the side door. He is breathing hard. He is holding a can of petrol. He empties the last of the can along the room. There is the stench of petrol from the rest of the house.
There are indistinct shouts from outside.
Scout runs back inside.

You're here. Thank God. We thought –

Arlo charges in.

Arlo The fire is really catching. We need water. Something. Fuck

Robin picks up the axe.

Scout What are you doing? Robin . . . What are you doing with that?

Robin smashes the axe into piano. He turns around slowly.

Robin Do you ever fantasise when you pass someone else's plate of food, and your hungry. Do you ever fantasise about just grabbing it. Eating it with your bare hands. You could. But you don't.

Beat.

Do you ever think? What's actually stopping you?

Scout What are you talking about?

He flicks the lighter. The flame illuminates his face.

Robin I jump. I choose.

Esme runs in, Tear streaked, panicked.

Esme We tried to stop her but she went in – she thought Robin was in there, we couldn't hold her back

Robin Who?

Esme Coby.

Another firework explodes. Filling the room with a flash of light.

Blackout.

Act Three

An hour later. Nearly dawn.

*Robin sits on the sofa. Coby lies with her head on his
lap. She is curled into him like an animal. Little of her is
visible.*

*Oliver stands on the other side of the room. He looks
pale. Sleepless. He stares at his brother.*

Oliver Wake her.

Robin I'll carry her to the car.

Oliver Wake her. Robin.

*Robin wakes Coby gently. She murmurs. Coby sits up
sleepily. Half her top has been cut away. Her arm is
viciously burnt.*

There is a car outside Coby. You need to go to hospital.
The others are leaving too. Your aunt is there. Time to go.

Coby shakes her head. Oliver kneels.

She's very worried, Coby. I said I would make sure . . .

Robin Hey . . . I'll come and see you tomorrow.

Coby Promise?

Robin Cross my heart.

*She stands unsteadily. Robin leads her out of the door.
Oliver takes in the room. Robin re enters.
The brothers stare at each other.*

Robin You look . . . terrible.

Oliver Do I? You don't look so hot yourself.

Robin I didn't know what she was going to do.

Oliver You left her unattended in a dangerous situation. You were high. Literally and egotistically off your face.

Robin She's not a child.

Oliver Actually. At fourteen technically she is.

Robin It was an accident

Oliver It was avoidable. Thank God I was already on my way. How would you have got her to hospital? What would you have done? What if you hadn't been able to put it out? What if she had been even more seriously hurt?

Robin hangs his head.

I love what you've done with the place, by the way. It's very. Understated.

Robin This is my half. Get out.

Oliver Were you seriously planning on burning this place down? A sacrifice of some sort, was it? Some sort of protest? 'Cause let me tell you. At best this is a shitty little riot.

Pause.

You've done them a favour, Robin. They were pulling the barn down anyway. And there's the insurance . . . The developers probably want to shake your grubby little hand.

Pause.

Can I have a drink?

Robin searches among the bottles. He finds some whisky. He holds it up to his brother. Oliver nods and reaches for it. Robin tries to pour it. His hands are shaking.

Just give it to me.

Robin No. I want to.

He pours the drink shakily. He hands it to Oliver, who sips it.
Pause.

It was Dad's drink, wasn't it? Whisky. A man's drink.

Oliver Aren't you having one?

Robin No. It tastes like tweed. Ugh.

Oliver You're forcing me to be like this, you know. It never had to be like this.

Robin You put her up to it. You must have.

Oliver No. Robin. I didn't. It was as much of a surprise to me as it –

Robin She wouldn't have done this to me –

Oliver Well. She has.

Robin This place was her, and you've sold it, you sold *her*.

Oliver *She* sold it, Robin. Anyway, she's dead. Nothing is 'her' any more.

Robin Fuck. You.

Oliver I gave you a month, Robin. I put them off for as long as I could. I gave you time. To say goodbye. I did.

Robin You made this happen. You made all of this happen. You put her in that place to die. You caged her. She was wild and you caged her. And it fucking killed her –

Oliver She ended up in the woods in her nightdress, Robin. She got pneumonia. She ended up in fucking hospital. They said the home was the best place for her. Them, not me.

Robin Bullshit. Here was the best place for her. I would have taken care of her till the end. I would have done. I would.

Oliver You'd have gone out on one of your jaunts and forgotten about her. You'd have come back to her in a pile of her own piss. You wouldn't have looked after her. You can barely look after yourself.

Beat.

When she started getting ill, what did you do? You got wrecked. You couldn't face it, so you spent half a year off your face, fighting anyone who tried to talk to you. Then when she goes missing, you get so drunk that you miss her arrive and miss her fucking killing herself, Robin.

Beat.

Her getting ill wasn't about her. It was about you. Like everything. Always about. You.

Beat.

She could have stayed here, you know. But she chose not to. She didn't trust you to look after her.

Robin She trusted me.

Oliver How, Robin? She didn't even tell you she was selling the house.

Robin is about to say something but can't.

Rat got your tongue?

Silence. He pours himself another drink, then one for Robin. He sets it next to him. Long pause.

It's so quiet here. Can practically hear your own heartbeat.

Robin Boom. Boom. Boom.

Oliver Boom. Boom.

Pause.

Robin How is work, by the way? Now you're . . . a shadow . . .

Oliver Difficult.

Robin Poor baby.

Oliver All my life. I've had you two mock what I do. Do you know what that's like? To play second fiddle to someone whose only skill is to actually play the fucking fiddle? You're the entertainment, That's all you are. A court jester in the court of her. This house was like its own country, the rest of the world didn't exist –

Robin You were away at school. Then university. You barely came home. How would you know what it was like –

Oliver Does that not occur to you that was why? That was why I never came home.

Robin I remember it good. I remember trees and light and not having to go to bed –

Oliver We were raised like dogs, with no sense of social responsibility, it was damaging. Look at you, you're proof. You have no context, you never have, your face is so firmly in a fucking piano that you pay no attention to the world around you. To the people around you. All you care about is your fucking art, which is a jumped-up way of only caring about yourself –

Robin I care. I care –

Oliver Was it caring of you to go on, if you'll excuse the pun, a *mother* of all benders when she started getting sick?

Robin I was scared –

Oliver And I wasn't?

94

Pause.

Exactly. No. Context.

Pause. Oliver takes in the room.

I worry about . . .

Robin About what?

Oliver The massive cunt you could become.

Robin So I'm not one already? Yikes . . . That's the nicest thing you've ever said to me.

Oliver You're one in training. A cub-scout cunt.

Robin laughs, Oliver smiles. It's the first one we've seen. Small pause.

Robin I know you don't think it. But I work here. I do. I work. I play.

Oliver It's not enough to be talented, Robin. It doesn't make you good.

Robin That's not what I meant –

Oliver It is. Look around. The world is full of talented derelicts –

Robin Said the politician to the fly –

Oliver What is your fucking problem with what I do? Can't you recognise that it's important?

Robin I don't trust it. Have you been out there lately, have you seen what people like you have *done*?

Oliver People like me? I'm trying to clean it up. It was people like Lily. It was that generation. They were told they could do what they want. Take what they want and there would be no consequences. Well, out there . . . is the consequence.

95

Robin I reject it.

Oliver Listen to me for one second, Robin, and I mean it, fucking listen to me, because I am sick of this pseudo-punk bohemian bullshit, sick of it –

Robin Go on then. Blow my mongrel mind.

Oliver Out there, the perfect storm is brewing. Climate change, population growth and resource shortages are cooking away together to create more famine, more droughts, more war then ever before. It's the beginning of the end, little brother. You're right to not like what you see. But doesn't that make it more important to engage, to participate? Put it this way . . . When you ask me what I want to be at this crucial time . . .

Beat.

Well . . . it's not a fucking musician.

Robin I didn't ask you.

Oliver This isn't about being different, Robin, it's about being good or not, it's about choosing whether to help just yourself or other people, it's not about taste, it's about fundamental fucking value, it's about the fact that it's wrong to lock yourself away in a house you did not work for and play the fucking piano, it's indulgent, it's *wrong*, it gives nothing back and now more then ever we need to *try* –

Robin MUSIC IS MY VALUE. Don't you get it? I'm not messing around. Sound means something to me. Like language did to Lily. I see so much ugliness out there, I find it hard to breathe. But making things transcends that. You can make beauty; make ships to cling to. That's why Lily . . . She was losing her words; she was losing her power to build things out of the dark. And I know you think it's indulgent. And I know you think we should all be arming up and fighting the common cause, but people have different 'whys' . . . You fight the ugliness in your way and me in mine . . .

Beat.

I wish you could see that. But you don't. She did and that was nothing against you, you were just . . . different.

He bows his head.

I miss her so much Ollie . . . I –

Oliver This isn't about her.

Robin She loved you. She loved you so much.

Oliver Look. Just don't. Don't.

Robin She. Did.

Beat.

Oliver You know the last time I saw her we fought. I swear she pretended to lose her mind halfway through. Just to. Get rid of me. She was sat there in hospital. Sat there in this sad little gown, with these tubes . . . And we still couldn't . . .

Beat.

That's why I was going to see her that morning. The morning she went missing. I wanted to say. Sorry.

Robin I didn't know that –

Oliver Just leave it, OK. It's done now. I don't want your –

Robin What?

Oliver Pity.

Robin It isn't pity for fuck's sake. You're sad too. Why don't you just admit it? You're sad too.

Robin tries to go to him. Oliver backs away.

Oliver Don't come near me, don't fucking touch me, you're toxic. Don't you get it? Had you been awake you could have stopped it . . . And because of that I never got to say sorry. Which will hang over me all my fucking life. All my fucking life, Robin. I gave you time. Did I have any? Did I fuck –

Pause. Oliver stares hard at Robin.

I remember when you were born. The blood. The screaming. You came early. I was at the hospital. I watched. From the door. They kept telling me to go. But I wouldn't. You nearly died.

Beat.

Robin I was born here.

Oliver You were born in hospital, Robin.

Robin Here. On that stain.

Oliver Robin, that stain is wine. You were born in London. Did she tell you that you were born here? Another tall fucking lie. You were brought up on mythology. Hollow mythology. That's why you're all stuck, all angry, a prince in the wrong story. A prince with a black eye.

Beat.

You were a brave little fucker. I saw you literally fight for your first breath. And look at you now. A coward.

Robin I'm not a coward.

Oliver You couldn't face the fact she was losing her mind. You obliterated yourself, you ran from it –

Robin I *was brave*. Wasn't that what her mouse books were about? About being brave –

Oliver Snoring upstairs as she topped herself, Robin. So very brave. Did you ever ask yourself why you got that drunk that day?

Robin struggles to compose himself.

Because you weren't strong enough to watch it happen over the years and months it would have taken. You were hiding from it. All this talk of being wild, animal, pure, that you both spouted over and over to justify nothing more than selfish carnal behaviour as far as I can see . . . Well, her decline, her decay was Mother Nature in fucking action, Robin, and you couldn't handle it. Admit it.
ADMIT IT.

Oliver pours himself another drink. He watches Robin.

This place is going. Just face the situation and live with it. I have to. Just face what you've fucking done. I have to. You're a drunk and a drug addict and a spoilt little boy. Your pathetic indulgence more or less killed her.

Robin seems about to say something.

Do you have something to say to that?

Pause.

Robin I like a margarita, but one at the very most, two I'm under the table . . .

Oliver winces. He steps back.

Two I'm under the table.

Oliver closes his eyes.

Three I'm under the . . .

Pause.

Oliver (*quietly*) Host.

Pause.

99

Robin How could you have known and not told me?

Oliver She didn't want you to know. I was only eleven, for fuck's sake.

Robin How did you know?

Oliver I saw the argument.

Robin What argument?

Oliver It's history, Robin. Ancient. Forget it.

Robin I deserve to know, don't I? Everything else is gone. Give me something. Something back. Please. Fucking please.

Oliver They'd been at a dinner party. I heard them come back. They'd clearly had a bad night. She was pissed and Gideon wasn't. She was jibing him. Riling. I shouldn't have listened. But eleven isn't that young.

Beat.

She wanted something from him that night. I don't know what. A rise. Something. He was so different to her. You don't remember but. No one else could have handled the . . .

He pauses.

When she couldn't get a rise out of him even after this had been going on for hours, he kept saying, let's go to bed, let's just go to bed . . . She resorted to . . . the big gun . . . You . . . you could have been anyone's. So you became just hers. Her bastard. Her blue-eyed boy.

Pause.

He got into the car. He didn't even want to go at first. But she kept taunting him. Be a man, be angry. It was snowing. The road looked like paper.

Beat.

Robin What month?

Oliver November.

Robin What day?

Oliver Don't do this.

Robin What fucking day?

Oliver The day he died.

> *Robin runs to the open garden doors. He pulls one shut as he leans outside vomiting.*
> *Behind the open door is Lily.*
> *Robin drags himself back in, obscuring her again with the door. When he shuts it Lily is gone.*
> *Silence.*

She was an artist to the end. Always trying to make something, anything happen. With whatever she could find.

> *Pause.*

Robin Why didn't you tell me?

Oliver Because it didn't matter.

Robin There were so many times you could have used that to . . .

Oliver You're my brother. I chose that. I choose that. You loved her so fiercely. Even if I couldn't have that with her, at least you could. I wanted to protect you just a little bit. From the world. Saw you be born, remember. Nothing takes that away. That . . . instinct . . .

> *Pause.*

That's when we left London. That's why we left London. She ran away here out of guilt. Out of grief. All that stuff she fed you about rejecting the world was a lie. About how he died was a lie. She ran away. Hounded by what happened. She ran into the woods. I never acknowledged it. And we never . . . recovered. But you were too little to remember any of it. So she rebuilt you. She failed as a novelist, as a wife, as a mother to me, so you became her work. Her piece of art.

Beat.

It is the hardest thing in my life. To have come from someone who is so foreign to me. A room with no lights. It scares me. She frightened me. But she made me want to fight. Seeing someone give up like that. Seeing someone. Just . . . retreat.

Beat.

The world is changing so fast. I know it scares you. But it might just be changing for the better. It might just be getting more democratic, more honest . . . free. It probably isn't. But we have to *try* . . . We have to fight. Not run away like her . . . There's hope yet. I believe that. I have to believe that.

Robin (*quietly*) Brave.

Oliver Being brave, Robin, is getting up and stumbling on. Choosing not to be fucked up. Choosing to try. Despite whatever has happened to you. It's marching on. It's believing.

Pause.

I think she sold the house so you wouldn't turn away. You have that same. Something. That same. Anger. Like you're not cut quite right for this world. Stuck in the wrong story. I think she knew that. Knew that you could disappear. Into these woods.

Beat.

I think the sale was . . . her gift. In a way. She burnt the woods down. Revealed you.

Pause.

Robin She loved you. I promise.

Oliver I really fucking miss her.

Oliver turns away. Silence.
After a moment Oliver comes to sit next to Robin. Robin turns towards the doors. The sky has been lightening slowly throughout the scene.

They turn towards it. Robin leans his head into Oliver's shoulder. Oliver sits stiffly for a moment then relaxes into it. Slowly his arm reaches around Robin.

The End.